Jesus

The
Open
Door

Jesus

The
Open
Door

Kenneth E. Hagin

Unless otherwise indicated, all Scripture quotations in this volume are from the *King James Version* of the Bible.

First Printing 1996

ISBN 0-89276-525-9

In the U.S. write:
Kenneth Hagin Ministries
P.O. Box 50126
Tulsa, OK 74150-0126

In Canada write:
Kenneth Hagin Ministries
P.O. Box 335, Station D,
Etobicoke (Toronto), Ontario
Canada, M9A 4X3

The Triumphant Church: Dominion Over All the Powers of Darkness
Healing Scriptures
Mountain-Moving Faith
Love: The Way to Victory
Biblical Keys to Financial Prosperity
Jesus — The Open Door
The Price Is Not Greater Than God's Grace (Mrs. Oretha Hagin)

MINIBOOKS (A partial listing)

* *The New Birth*
* *Why Tongues?*
* *In Him*
* *God's Medicine*
* *You Can Have What You Say*
* *Don't Blame God*
* *How To Keep Your Healing*
  The Bible Way To Receive the Holy Spirit
  I Went to Hell
  How To Walk in Love
  The Precious Blood of Jesus
* *Love Never Fails*
  How God Taught Me About Prosperity

BOOKS BY KENNETH HAGIN JR.

* *Man's Impossibility — God's Possibility*
  Because of Jesus
  How To Make the Dream God Gave You Come True
  The Life of Obedience
  Forget Not!
  God's Irresistible Word
  Healing: Forever Settled
  Don't Quit! Your Faith Will See You Through
  The Untapped Power in Praise
  Listen to Your Heart
  What Comes After Faith?
  Speak to Your Mountain!
  Come Out of the Valley!
  It's Your Move!
  God's Victory Plan
  Another Look at Faith
  How To Live Worry-Free
  Soaring With the Eagles

MINIBOOKS (A partial listing)

* *Faith Worketh by Love*
* *Seven Hindrances to Healing*
* *The Past Tense of God's Word*
  Faith Takes Back What the Devil's Stolen
  How To Be a Success in Life
  Unforgiveness
  Ministering to the Brokenhearted

*These titles are also available in Spanish. Information about other foreign translations of several of the above titles (i.e., Finnish, French, German, Indonesian, Polish, Russian, etc.) may be obtained by writing to: Kenneth Hagin Ministries, P.O. Box 50126, Tulsa, Oklahoma 74150-0126.

Contents

Chapter 1
Jesus' Character
And Work Revealed

. . . to the angel of the church in Philadelphia write; These things saith he that is HOLY, he that is TRUE, he that hath THE KEY OF DAVID, HE THAT OPENETH, and no man shutteth; and SHUTTETH, and no man openeth;

. . . behold, I have set before thee AN OPEN DOOR, and NO MAN CAN SHUT IT. . . .

— Revelation 3:7,8

The Lord sets before us wonderful doors of opportunities, blessings, and provisions. What's more, they are not *closed* doors, but they are wide *open* doors of divine blessing.

As we walk through the Lord's open doors, we receive divine riches that He has prepared for us because of our inheritance in Christ.

During the Apostle John's exile on the Isle of Patmos, the Lord first gave him the revelation of Jesus as the One who opens doors. In fact, the entire Book of Revelation is the vision and revelation of Jesus Christ

1

and was written when Jesus appeared to John while he was in the Spirit on the Lord's day.

During this time, the Lord also gave John messages for the seven churches that existed in Asia Minor at that time. In Revelation 3:8, Jesus told John that He was setting an open door before the Philadelphia Church, a door that no *man* could open or shut.

However, the messages Jesus gave John for the churches also teach us a lesson. They contain messages from God to us. For example, in Revelation chapters 2 and 3, notice something that Jesus repeated over and over again: *"He that hath an ear, let him hear what the Spirit saith unto the churches"* (Rev. 2:7,11,17,29; 3:6,13,22).

According to *The Amplified Bible*, Jesus was actually saying, "He who is able to hear, let him listen to and heed what the [Holy] Spirit says to the assemblies (churches)."

I believe that includes those of us living today. We too need to hear what the Spirit is saying to the Church. We *are* the Church — the Body of Christ.

Jesus Is the Holy One and the True One

What is the message for the Body of Christ today? It is found in Revelation 3:7 and 8.

The Lord Jesus Christ is speaking in these verses. We know Jesus is the One speaking because verse 7 says, *". . . These things SAITH HE THAT IS HOLY, HE THAT IS TRUE . . . HE THAT OPENETH. . . ."* Jesus is the One who qualifies as the Holy One and the True One.

By saying this, Jesus is giving us a description of Himself. He is revealing His *character* to us. What is His character?

Jesus is *holy* and *true*. Those qualities are aspects of His character.

Therefore, the first thing Jesus revealed about His character in Revelation 3:7 is that He is holy and true. You see, Jesus could say He is *holy* because no fault was found in Him by God, by man, or by the devil. We will also see why Jesus could say of Himself that He is *true*.

God Found No Fault in Jesus

You remember that Jesus was baptized by John in the Jordan River. As He came straightway up out of the water, the Spirit of God descended upon Him in bodily shape and form like a dove.

Then a Voice spoke from Heaven, saying, "*. . . Thou art my beloved Son; IN THEE I AM WELL PLEASED*" (Luke 3:22). Therefore, God found no fault in Him. In fact, God the Father said He was well pleased with Jesus.

Then God also spoke from Heaven on another occasion about Jesus. You remember when Jesus took Peter, James, and John and went up to the Mount of Transfiguration. The Bible says that the cloud of God's glory overshadowed them.

MATTHEW 17:5
5 . . . A BRIGHT CLOUD overshadowed them: and behold A VOICE OUT OF THE CLOUD, which said, THIS IS MY BELOVED SON, IN WHOM I AM WELL PLEASED; hear ye him.

Jesus pleased God because He was and is the Holy One. In other words, God found no fault in Him.

Man Found No Fault in Jesus

Men tried to find fault in Jesus, but they couldn't find any sin in Him. Men even examined Jesus before the courts of men; they tried to find fault in Him and trap Him in His words. But they couldn't find any error in Him because His character is pure, holy, and true.

In fact, throughout His ministry, men brought Jesus before human courts of public opinion and judgment. For example, the Word of God tells us that the Pharisees thought surely they could challenge Jesus and that He would say something that would get Him in trouble with the Roman government.

The Pharisees said, "We want to ask You a question. Should we pay taxes to Caesar or not?" Well, that is a question some people ask even today, isn't it? People will get in trouble even in our day if they don't pay their taxes.

The Pharisees thought they would catch Jesus in an error. If He said, "Yes, you must pay taxes to Caesar," then He would be in trouble with the religious folks.

But if He said, "No, you should not pay taxes to Caesar," then He would be in trouble with the government. However, Jesus answered in such a way that no fault could be found in Him by anyone.

MARK 12:13-17
13 And they send unto him [Jesus] certain of the Pharisees and of the Herodians, TO CATCH HIM IN HIS WORDS.

**14 And when they were come, they say unto him, Master, we know that THOU ART TRUE, and carest for no man: for thou regardest not the person of men, but teachest the way of God IN TRUTH: Is it lawful to give tribute to Caesar, or not?
15 Shall we give, or shall we not give? But he, knowing their hypocrisy, said unto them, Why tempt ye me? bring me a penny, that I may see it.
16 And they brought it. And he saith unto them, Whose is this image and superscription? And they said unto him, Caesar's.
17 And Jesus answering said unto them, Render to Caesar the things that are Caesar's, and to God the things that are God's. And THEY MARVELLED AT HIM.**

You see, even the Pharisees, the strictest religious sect of the day, could find no fault in Jesus. Matthew's Gospel says, *"When they had heard these words, they marvelled, and left him, and went their way"* (Matt. 22:22). Jesus, the Holy One, could not be found in error.

Then the Sadducees had their try at Him. The Sadducees did not believe in the resurrection from the dead, nor did they believe in angels or spirits. So they came to ask Jesus a question concerning Jewish Law, hoping to catch Him in an error.

**MARK 12:18-27
18 Then come unto him the Sadducees, which say there is no resurrection; and they asked him, saying,
19 Master, Moses wrote unto us, If a man's brother die, and leave his wife behind him, and leave no children, that his brother should take his wife,**

and raise up seed unto his brother.
20 Now there were seven brethren: and the first took a wife, and dying left no seed.
21 And the second took her, and died, neither left he any seed: and the third likewise.
22 And the seven had her, and left no seed: last of all the woman died also.
23 In the resurrection therefore, when they shall rise, whose wife shall she be of them? for the seven had her to wife.
24 And Jesus answering said unto them, Do ye not therefore err, because ye know not the scriptures, neither the power of God?
25 For when they shall rise from the dead, they neither marry, nor are given in marriage; but are as the angels which are in heaven.
26 And as touching the dead, that they rise: have ye not read in the book of Moses, how in the bush God spake unto him, saying, I am the God of Abraham, and the God of Isaac, and the God of Jacob?
27 He is not the God of the dead, but the God of the living: ye therefore do greatly err.

Jesus answered with such wisdom and authority that the Sadducees could find no fault in Him either. The officers of the chief priests and the Pharisees also wanted to question Jesus to try to trap Him in His words. But they could not.

No wonder they came back and reported, *"Never man spake like this man"* (John 7:45,46). Why? Because Jesus is the Holy One. He is the True One, and there is no fault or flaw in His character whatsoever.

On another occasion, the religious authorities of the day tried to trap Jesus by demanding on what authority He performed His miracles.

MARK 11:27-29,33
27 And they come again to Jerusalem: and as he was walking in the temple, there come to him the chief priests, and the scribes, and the elders,
28 And say unto him, By what authority doest thou these things? and who gave thee this authority to do these things?
29 And Jesus answered and said unto them, I will also ask of you one question, and answer me, and I will tell you by what authority I do these things....
33 And they answered and said unto Jesus, We cannot tell. And Jesus answering saith unto them, Neither do I tell you by what authority I do these things.

No matter what the religious leaders tried to do to trap Jesus, they could not catch Him in His words because He is the Holy One.

No fault could be found in Him by man because His character was and is flawless.

Even when Jesus stood before a human tribunal to be crucified, man could find no charge against Him. Even Judas, his accuser, could find no fault in Him. Judas said, "... *I have sinned in that I have betrayed the innocent blood...*" (Matt. 27:4).

Pilate asked the crowd of Jesus' accusers: "... *what evil hath he done?...*" (Matt. 27:23). Pilate had no accusation to bring against Jesus, because Jesus had done nothing worthy of death.

MATTHEW 27:24
24 When Pilate saw that he could prevail nothing, but that rather a tumult was made, he took water,

and washed his hands before the multitude, saying, I am innocent of the blood of THIS JUST PERSON: see ye to it.

In front of every single human tribunal, no fault was found in Jesus by man. His character stood the test of man because He is holy and true.

Satan Found No Fault in Jesus

The devil tried to find fault in Jesus too. In Matthew 4, Jesus was led by the Spirit into the wilderness to be tempted of the devil.

After Jesus had fasted forty days and nights, Satan came to Him and said, "If You are the Son of God, command that these stones be made bread" (Matt. 4:3). Jesus answered, "*. . . It is written, Man shall not live by bread alone, but by every word that proceedeth out of the mouth of God*" (Matt. 4:4).

Satan was trying to tempt Jesus and trap Him in His words. But Jesus rebuked Him with the Word of God, saying, "*It is written . . .*" (Matt. 4:4,7,10).

Then Satan took Jesus to the highest point of the temple, and said, "If You are the Son of God, cast Yourself down. God will save You" (Matt. 4:6). Satan even quoted the Scriptures to try to trap Jesus with the Word.

MATTHEW 4:6
6 . . . If thou be the Son of God, cast thyself down: FOR IT IS WRITTEN, He shall give his angels charge concerning thee: and in their hands they shall bear thee up, lest at any time thou dash thy foot against a stone.

Satan can quote Scripture when it suits his purposes to do so. But Jesus rightly divided the Word, saying, ". . . *IT IS WRITTEN again, Thou shalt not tempt the Lord thy God*" (Matt. 4:7). Therefore, Satan could not find any fault in Jesus.

Then Satan took Jesus up on a high mountain and showed Him all the kingdoms of earth in a moment of time. Satan told Jesus if He would fall down and worship him, he would give Jesus all the kingdoms of the world with all their glory.

Jesus answered him, ". . . *Get thee hence, Satan: for it is written, Thou shalt worship the Lord thy God, and him only shalt thou serve*" (Matt. 4:10).

Satan could not trick Jesus with any of these temptations. Jesus stood steadfast by declaring what the Word said. Jesus whipped Satan with the Word. Jesus' character stood the test of temptations and trials because He is the Holy One and the True One. Satan couldn't find any fault in Jesus.

No fault was found in Jesus by God, by man, or by the devil because Jesus' character is holy and true.

Jesus Is the Faithful and True Witness

You see, Jesus could also say of Himself in Revelation 3:7 that He is the True One because no flaw was found in His character. We know that Jesus' character is faithful and true because that is one of His Names in eternity.

REVELATION 19:11
11 And I saw heaven opened, and behold a white horse; and HE THAT SAT UPON HIM WAS

**CALLED FAITHFUL AND TRUE, and in righteous-
ness he doth judge and make war.**

Then also in the Book of Revelation, Jesus Himself
revealed something else about His character. He
revealed that He is the Faithful and True Witness.

REVELATION 3:14
**14 And unto the angel of the church of the
Laodiceans write; These things saith the Amen,
THE FAITHFUL AND TRUE WITNESS, the beginning of the creation of God.**

Why could the Bible say that Jesus is the Faithful
and True Witness? Because Jesus faithfully represented
the Father. Remember that Jesus said, ". . . *he that
hath seen me hath seen the Father . . ."* (John 14:9).

In fact, in His earthly walk, Jesus' testimony about
the Father God was so faithful and true that you could
look at Jesus and see what God is like. You could see
the Father's character and nature in Jesus. Acts 10:38
says that Jesus ". . . *went about doing good, and healing all that were oppressed of the devil; for God was
with him."*

We know Jesus is a true witness because He said,
*"For I came down from heaven, not to do mine own will,
but the will of him that sent me"* (John 6:38). The defini-
tion of the word "true" is *honest, steadfast, honorable,
just, right,* and *faithful.*

Jesus was honest, steadfast, honorable, just, right,
and faithful to carry out the Father's will on the earth.
Jesus said, "The words I speak unto you, they are not

Mine, but they are My Father's" (John 14:10). Jesus was a faithful and true witness of the Father in every situation.

> **JOHN 12:49,50**
> **49 For I have not spoken of myself; but the Father which sent me, he gave me a commandment, what I should say, and what I should speak.**
> **50 And I know that his commandment is life everlasting: whatsoever I speak therefore, even as the Father said unto me, so I speak.**

Jesus was faithful and true to speak only what He heard from the Father. He faithfully represented the Heavenly Father even in His words.

Many times, people talk about political people and television personalities who stand at the forefront in different areas of our culture. The question is often asked, "Just what is that person really like?"

For example, sometimes interviewers ask about those who are running for president or some other public office, "What is he really like?" People can get one image of the candidate in public, but they want to know if the person is really like that all the time.

Sometimes folks may wonder and ask the question, "What is God really like?"

But if you really want to know what God is like, just look at Jesus (Acts 10:38). If you want to hear God talking, listen to Jesus. If you want to see God at work, look at Jesus. Jesus faithfully represented the Father God in every way to the people.

Jesus Is the Authorized One —
He Holds the Key of David

Isaiah 22:22
**22 And the key of the house of David will I lay
upon his shoulder; so he shall open, and none shall
shut; and he shall shut. . . .**

Jesus is the Authorized One — He is the One who
has the key of David. In the Scriptures, keys are often
used as a symbol of power and authority. Giving keys to
a person signifies that you are entrusting him with an
important charge. God has entrusted Him that is faithful and true.

God had made a covenant with David, promising
that a descendant of David would come and always sit
on the throne of the house of Israel. That was literally
fulfilled in the coming of the Lord Jesus Christ with His
ascension on High to sit at the Father's right hand
(Heb. 1:3).

JEREMIAH 33:17,20,21
**17 For thus saith the Lord; DAVID SHALL NEVER
WANT A MAN TO SIT UPON THE THRONE OF
THE HOUSE OF ISRAEL; . . .**
**20 Thus saith the Lord, If ye can break my
covenant of the day, and my covenant of the night,
and that there should not be day and night in
their season;**
**21 Then may also my covenant be broken with
David my servant, that HE SHOULD NOT HAVE A
SON TO REIGN UPON HIS THRONE. . . .**

God was referring to Jesus when He said that. Jesus was not born of natural seed even though Joseph, Jesus' earthly father, was of the house and lineage of David (Luke 1:27).

The Bible says the power of the Most High overshadowed Mary (Luke 1:35). Therefore, Jesus was born of supernatural seed; *supernaturally* Jesus was of the seed and lineage of David.

> **LUKE 1:30-33**
> **30 And the angel said unto her, Fear not, Mary: for thou hast found favour with God.**
> **31 And, behold, thou shalt conceive in thy womb, and bring forth a son, and shalt call his name JESUS.**
> **32 He shall be great, and shall be called the Son of the Highest: and THE LORD GOD SHALL GIVE UNTO HIM THE THRONE OF HIS FATHER DAVID:**
> **33 And HE SHALL REIGN OVER THE HOUSE OF JACOB FOR EVER; and OF HIS KINGDOM THERE SHALL BE NO END.**

You see, David ruled over Israel in the natural (2 Sam. 5:5). But it was prophesied that the Christ would come from the house of David, and He would rule over His people supernaturally — He would sit on the throne of David and reign forever. Therefore, the covenant God made with David as recorded in the Old Testament was fulfilled in Jesus (Ps. 89:3,4,34,35; 132:11,12; Jer. 33:20,21).

This was later confirmed in the New Testament when Zechariah prophesied about the Savior who would come from the house of David.

LUKE 1:68,69
**68 Blessed be the Lord God of Israel; for he hath
visited and redeemed his people,**
**69 And hath raised up an HORN OF SALVATION
for us in the HOUSE OF HIS SERVANT DAVID.**

That's talking about Jesus Christ who would be
given the key of David. According to one commentator,
the key of David "implies the royal power and authority
of Davidic dynasty or kingdom. . . . In the New Testament this power is lodged in the risen Christ." [1]

We see in the Scriptures that Jesus is the One who
was given royal power and authority. In other words,
Jesus Christ was to ultimately carry on or fulfill the
reign of the house of David *supernaturally* as the Messiah and Lord.

Then on the Day of Pentecost, Peter stood up and
spoke to the 120 believers who were gathered in the
Upper Room that day.

He confirmed the fact that Jesus Christ is the One
who came to sit on the throne of David to rule His people.

ACTS 2:29,30,34-36
**29 Men and brethren, let me freely speak unto you
of the patriarch David, that he is both dead and
buried, and his sepulchre is with us unto this day.**
**30 Therefore being a prophet, and knowing that
God had sworn with an oath to him, that of the
fruit of his loins, according to the flesh, HE
WOULD RAISE UP CHRIST TO SIT ON HIS
THRONE; . . .**
**34 For David is not ascended into the heavens:
but he saith himself, The Lord said unto my Lord,
Sit thou on my right hand,**

**35 Until I make thy foes thy footstool.
36 Therefore let all the house of Israel know assuredly, that God hath made that same Jesus, whom ye have crucified, BOTH LORD and CHRIST.**

According to different Bible commentaries, in ancient Eastern countries, keys were sometimes carried over the shoulder as a symbol of power and authority.

This is fulfilled in Jesus' eternal reign, because the Old Testament Scriptures predicted that one day all government and authority would be under the Messiah's dominion. In other words, "the government shall be upon his shoulder."

**ISAIAH 9:6
6 For unto us a child is born, unto us a son is given: and THE GOVERNMENT SHALL BE UPON HIS SHOULDER: and his name shall be called Wonderful, Counsellor, The mighty God, The everlasting Father, The Prince of Peace.**

Therefore, talking about Jesus' eternal reign, the key of the house of David symbolizes Jesus' authority and power to "sustain the government on his shoulders." ²

**1 CORINTHIANS 15:24
24 Then cometh the end, when he shall have delivered up the kingdom to God, even the Father; when he shall have put down ALL RULE and ALL AUTHORITY and POWER.**

Our text scripture, Revelation 3:7, says that Jesus was given the key of David, indicating that all authority was given to Him. That's what the Bible means when it says, *". . . the government shall be upon his shoulder. . . ."*

As the Christ and Lord, Jesus literally brought to pass Old Testament prophecy to rule and reign forever and ever, which fulfilled the Davidic Covenant. Jesus was given the key of David to spiritually sit on David's throne and rule and reign over His people Israel — and of His kingdom there shall be no end.

> **LUKE 1:32,33**
> **32 He shall be great, and shall be called the Son of the Highest: and the Lord God shall give unto him THE THRONE OF HIS FATHER DAVID:**
> **33 And HE SHALL REIGN OVER THE HOUSE OF JACOB FOR EVER; and OF HIS KINGDOM THERE SHALL BE NO END.**

Now you can see why Jesus is the One who has the authority and ability to open and shut doors.

> **REVELATION 3:7**
> **7 . . . These things saith he that is holy, he that is true, HE THAT HATH THE KEY OF DAVID, he that OPENETH, and no man shutteth; and SHUTTETH, and no man openeth.**

What Jesus opens, no man can shut. Jesus also has the authority to shut doors, and what He shuts no man can open. The key of David means that Jesus has authority no man possesses.

Isaiah also prophesied about Jesus' authority to open and close doors. Notice that Isaiah also uses the phrase "the key of David" in connection with Jesus' authority. It is interesting that Isaiah also prophesied that God would "lay the key of David on Jesus' shoulder," talking about Jesus' reign.

ISAIAH 22:22
22 And the KEY OF THE HOUSE OF DAVID WILL I LAY UPON HIS SHOULDER; so HE SHALL OPEN, and none shall shut; and HE SHALL SHUT, and none shall open.

The key of the house of David can also be understood as the power and authority to give access to God and to eternal life. We know that Jesus is the Authorized One giving us access to God and to eternal life because the Scripture says, *"For there is one God, and one mediator between God and men, the man Christ Jesus"* (1 Tim. 2:5).

Also, Jesus Himself said, "I have the keys of hell and death." No *man* has authority over hell and death.

REVELATION 1:18
18 I am he that liveth, and was dead; and, behold, I am alive for evermore, Amen; and have THE KEYS OF HELL AND OF DEATH.

Thank God, Jesus went down to the dark regions of the domain of death and led captivity captive (Eph. 4:8,9). He took the keys of hell and death away from Satan and arose on that glad Resurrection morning long ago — the Victor over death, hell, and the grave!

When Jesus arose from the dead, He went to tell His disciples. He gave them the revelation that He is the Authorized One because all power in Heaven and earth was given unto Him. The government is upon His shoulders! He alone has the key of David.

> **MATTHEW 28:9,10,16-18**
> **9   And as they went to tell his disciples, behold, Jesus met them, saying, All hail. And they came and held him by the feet, and worshipped him.**
> **10 Then said Jesus unto them, Be not afraid: go tell my brethren that they go into Galilee, and there shall they see me. . . .**
> **16 Then the eleven disciples went away into Galilee, into a mountain where Jesus had appointed them.**
> **17 And when they saw him, they worshipped him: but some doubted.**
> **18 And Jesus came and spake unto them, saying, ALL POWER IS GIVEN UNTO ME IN HEAVEN AND IN EARTH.**

Jesus told His disciples that all power had been given unto Him in Heaven and in earth. How could all power be given to Jesus? Because He is the Holy One; He is the True One; He is the Faithful and the True Witness.

He is the Authorized One — possessing the key of David — the key of power and authority forever. He is authorized to open and close doors. And Jesus has the keys of death and hell (Rev. 1:18).

> **REVELATION 5:1-5**
> **1   And I saw in the right hand of him that sat on the throne a book written within and on the back-side, SEALED WITH SEVEN SEALS.**
> **2   And I saw a strong angel proclaiming with a loud voice, WHO IS WORTHY TO OPEN THE BOOK, and to loose the seals thereof?**

> **3** And NO MAN IN HEAVEN, NOR IN EARTH,
> NEITHER UNDER THE EARTH, WAS ABLE TO
> OPEN THE BOOK, NEITHER TO LOOK THEREON.
> **4** And I wept much, because NO MAN WAS
> FOUND WORTHY TO OPEN AND TO READ THE
> BOOK, neither to look thereon.
> **5** And one of the elders saith unto me, Weep not:
> BEHOLD, THE LION OF THE TRIBE OF JUDA,
> the Root of David, HATH PREVAILED TO OPEN
> THE BOOK, and to loose the seven seals thereof.

Jesus is the only One worthy to open the book
sealed with seven seals. Why? Because He is the Holy
One, the True One, and the Faithful and True Witness.
He is the Authorized One; He holds the key of David
and the keys of death and hell.

Jesus' Twofold Work

Actually, our text scripture, Revelation 3:7, reveals
two things to us: Jesus' *character* and Jesus' *work*.
We've seen His character. But in this passage, we also
see something concerning *the work* that the Holy One
and the True One does.

> **REVELATION 3:7**
> **7** . . . to the angel of the church in Philadelphia
> write; These things saith he that is HOLY, he that
> is TRUE, he that hath THE KEY OF DAVID, HE
> THAT OPENETH, and no man shutteth; and
> SHUTTETH, and no man openeth.

Jesus' work is twofold in nature: He opens and
shuts doors. He said about Himself, "I am He that
openeth and no man shutteth. I am He that *shutteth*

and no man openeth." Opening and shutting doors is symbolic of Jesus' authority. The symbol of the key is a picture of His authority.

Therefore, one aspect of Jesus' work is to open and shut doors. Actually, in the Gospels, Jesus called Himself the Door. He said, *"I AM THE DOOR: by me if any man enter in, he shall be saved, and shall go in and out, and find pasture"* (John 10:9).

So we see that Jesus is the door to salvation. Jesus is the open Door to all who will believe and receive Him. The Bible says, *"Neither is there salvation in any other: for there is none other name under heaven given among men, whereby we must be saved"* (Acts 4:12).

Well, that's enough to shout about right there! Then in Revelation 3:8, Jesus went on to say, ". . . *behold, I have set before thee AN OPEN DOOR. . . ."* Everyone is invited to enter through the open door of salvation.

Jesus is not shutting His doors of blessings on His people! His doors of blessings are open to all, praise God. All may enter in through those open doors.

Jesus is also the closer of doors. There are some doors that will eventually close if people refuse to accept Jesus and His open doors of blessing.

Can *You* Shut Doors Jesus Opens for You?

It is important to know that when Jesus opens a door for you, no man can shut it. Your momma can't shut it; your daddy can't shut it; your pastor can't shut a door that Jesus opens for you.

Actually, *you* are the only one who can in effect shut the doors of God's blessing on your life. How? By a lack of understanding or by disobedience. You see, there is a God-ward side and a man-ward side to everything we receive from God.

Many times folks want to leave it all up to God. They say, "Whatever I need, I know the Lord will send it. If I need healing, He will send that. Whatever it is, God will just send it."

That sounds good, and that sounds religious. But, really, putting it in the context of what Jesus said, it isn't true. Why? Because when it comes to the provisions of God, Jesus has already set before us an *open* door.

> **EPHESIANS 1:3**
> 3 **Blessed be the God and Father of our Lord Jesus Christ, who hath BLESSED US WITH ALL SPIRITUAL BLESSINGS IN HEAVENLY PLACES in Christ.**

In other words, the open door of God's blessings is already there for us to enter into because God provided us with *all* spiritual blessings in Christ Jesus. What are some of Jesus' open doors to God's blessings?

Well, there is the open door of salvation, the door of service and opportunity, the door of divine healing, the door of utterance, and the door of financial blessing. Then Jesus also opens for us the door of Heaven.

Since Jesus has opened wide His doors of blessing for us, then the responsibility is *ours* whether or not we ever enter through those open doors.

Throughout the Bible, from the Old Testament right on through to the last page of the New Testament, you will find again and again where the Word of God puts the responsibility for receiving the blessings of God upon each individual person.

For example, God said, ". . . *CHOOSE YOU this day whom ye will serve . . .*" (Joshua 24:15). He leaves the choice up to us. He didn't say, "I am going to choose for you whom you *must* serve." No, He said *you* choose whom you *will* serve.

Then in the Book of Revelation the Word of God said, ". . . *the Spirit and the bride say, Come. And let him that heareth say, Come . . . WHOSOEVER WILL, let him take the water of life freely*" (Rev. 22:17).

Notice that it says "whosoever." That means each individual person must make the choice for himself to enter through God's doors of blessings!

The blessings of God and everything else God wants you to have are not going to automatically fall on you like ripe cherries off a tree.

No, there are some things you will have to do to receive God's blessings and provisions. *You* have a part to play in receiving from God.

Jesus has done His part because He's already opened those doors of blessing. And since Jesus has set before you open doors that no man can shut, it's up to *you* to walk through them!

I don't know about you, but I like that word "open." Not *closed* — not *shut* — but *open*. Thank God for the doors of blessing and provision that Jesus has already opened and set before us!

Wouldn't it be a pity to come to the end of life's journey never having enjoyed God's promises or provisions — even though they were already prepared for us? Therefore, we need to see what the Bible says about each door so we can know if we are walking through the doors that Jesus has so freely opened for us.

---

[1] *Wycliffe Bible Encyclopedia,* Vol. 2. (Chicago, Illinois: Moody Press, 1975), p. 988.

[2] *The Bethany Parallel Commentary of the Old Testament* (Minneapolis, Minnesota: Bethany House Publishers, 1985), p. 1390.

Chapter 2
Jesus: The Open Door
Of Salvation

Jesus has opened the door of salvation to every person. Thank God, Jesus has opened the door of salvation that no one can shut — unless the person himself refuses to walk through that open door by not receiving Jesus Christ as his Savior.

What does it mean that Jesus is the Door to salvation? Remember, Jesus said, *"I am the door: by me if any man enter in, he shall be saved . . ."* (John 10:9).

Then in Hebrews 10:20, the Bible says, *"By a new and living way, which he* [Jesus] *hath consecrated for us, through the veil, that is to say, his flesh."* In other words, by shedding His blood on the Cross at Calvary, Jesus opened the door of salvation to every person who would ever live on this earth.

You see, when Jesus died and shed His blood for the remission of our sins, the curtain that separated the Holy of Holies from the Holy place was rent in two. That partition separated man from the Holy of Holies where the Presence of God dwelt under the Old Covenant.

HEBREWS 10:19,20 (*Amplified*)
19 Therefore, brethren, since we have full freedom and confidence to enter into the [Holy of]

Holies [by the power and virtue] in the blood of Jesus,
20 By this fresh (new) and living way which He initiated and dedicated and opened for us through the separating curtain [veil of the Holy of Holies], that is, THROUGH HIS FLESH.

Once that partition was rent by the sacrifice of Jesus' own body on the Cross of Calvary, the Presence of God was no longer contained in a man-made tabernacle. By the sacrifice of Jesus, the Presence of God came to dwell in every person who would receive Jesus Christ as his Savior (John 14:23).

Jesus Himself Is the Door

That's why Jesus Himself is the Door of salvation, because He made the way for all people to be saved by His sacrificing Himself. And Jesus called Himself the Door. In fact, there is no other door through which we can receive salvation or eternal life (Acts 4:12).

In John chapter 10, we see that Jesus is both the Door and the Good Shepherd. In verse 11, Jesus called Himself the Good Shepherd. The Good Shepherd lays down His life for the sheep. The sheep know His voice and follow Him.

JOHN 10:1-11
1   Verily, verily, I say unto you, He that entereth not by THE DOOR into the sheepfold, but climbeth up some other way, the same is a thief and a robber.
2   But he that entereth in by THE DOOR is the

shepherd of the sheep.
3   TO HIM [the Shepherd] **the porter openeth; and
THE SHEEP HEAR HIS VOICE: and he calleth his
own sheep by name, and leadeth them out.**
**4   And when he putteth forth his own sheep, he
goeth before them, and the sheep follow him: FOR
THEY KNOW HIS VOICE.**
**5   And a stranger will they not follow, but will
flee from him: for they know not the voice of
strangers.**
**6   This parable spake Jesus unto them: but they
understood not what things they were which he
spake unto them.**
**7   Then said Jesus unto them again, Verily, verily,
I say unto you, I AM THE DOOR of the sheep.**
**8   All that ever came before me are thieves and
robbers: but the sheep did not hear them.**
**9   I AM THE DOOR: BY ME IF ANY MAN ENTER
IN, HE SHALL BE SAVED, and shall go in and out,
and find pasture.**
**10 The thief cometh not, but for to steal, and to
kill, and to destroy: I am come that they might
have life, and that they might have it more abundantly.**
**11 I AM THE GOOD SHEPHERD: the good shep-
herd giveth his life for the sheep.**

Because Jesus is the Good Shepherd, the porter
opens the door to Him. Jesus the Door to salvation protects the sheep so that no thief or robber can come
through Him to get into the sheepfold. Therefore, Jesus
is both the Door of salvation and the Good Shepherd
who protects His sheep.

So, you see, Jesus the Door of salvation has already
made a way for the redemption of every person who

would ever live on this earth. But each person must walk through that door of salvation for himself. God puts the responsibility on each person whether or not he will receive Jesus Christ as his Savior.

Salvation Defined

When we talk about the door of salvation, we are talking about Jesus providing us with the new birth and the remission of sin. Because of Jesus' sacrifice on the Cross for us, we can receive eternal life and become new creatures in Christ Jesus (2 Cor. 5:17).

But, friend, there is more involved in salvation than just the new birth and the remission of sins. That's part of salvation, but that isn't all of it.

You see, much more than the new birth is implied in this word "salvation."

> **ROMANS 1:16**
> **16 For I am not ashamed of the gospel of Christ: for it is THE POWER OF GOD unto SALVATION to every one that believeth; to the Jew first, and also to the Greek.**

A note in the margin of my Bible points out that the Hebrew and Greek words for salvation imply not only the idea of forgiveness of sin, but also of healing and health. The word "salvation" actually means *healing, health, safety, deliverance, soundness,* and *wholeness.*

"Whosoever will" may come through this door of salvation! Each individual person must choose for himself whether he will enter into the blessings and benefits that salvation provides for him. The benefits of salvation include healing, health, safety, deliverance, soundness, and wholeness.

> **REVELATION 22:17**
> **17 And the Spirit and the bride say, Come. And let him that heareth say, Come. And let him that is athirst come. And WHOSOEVER WILL, let him take the water of life** [salvation] **freely.**

Dear friend, that door is still open, but one of these days it will be shut — and then it will be too late (2 Cor. 6:2; Gen. 6:3). You are the one who decides if you will ever walk through the door of salvation; you alone decide where you will spend eternity.

Now some folks seem to think they can decide where other people will spend eternity. In other words, if some folks had anything to do with it, they wouldn't let certain people through the door of salvation! They would shut the door of salvation on them if they could.

And if some folks had anything to do with opening or closing the door of salvation, they would have certain rules, regulations, and requirements others would have to meet before they could enter through the door of salvation.

For example, some people feel that if you don't belong to their particular congregation, you can't be saved. Others believe that you have to be baptized in water by a certain formula before you can be saved. But I'm glad that all such human thinking is in error.

In fact, through the years, I've had several people tell me that I won't go to Heaven when I die because I don't belong to their little group. Those folks tried to shut the door of salvation on me, but Jesus opened that door and no man can shut it!

Thank God, I found the open door to salvation through Jesus, and after I was born again, I knew I was already on the other side of that door! I was saved! I didn't have to ask those folks whether I could get in that door or not — Jesus settled that issue once and for all by the sacrifice of Himself!

And the door of salvation is still open to this day. It will not always be open, but it is still open now. But there will come a day when the door of salvation will be closed; it will be too late to accept Jesus Christ as Lord and Savior.

The Shut Door of the Ark

We've talked about the positive side — the doors that Jesus opens. But, you see, He not only opens doors, the Bible also says He shuts doors. Jesus is the One who *". . . openeth, and no man shutteth; and shutteth, and no man openeth"* (Rev. 3:7).

What are some of the doors that Jesus shuts? Well, for one thing, He shuts the doors of the floodgates of wrath. Go back to the Book of Genesis, and you'll see a type of what I mean.

The Bible said that in the days of Noah, the Lord made a covenant with Noah: *"But with thee will I establish my covenant; and thou shalt come into the ark, thou, and thy sons, and thy wife, and thy sons' wives with thee"* (Gen. 6:18).

Noah obeyed God and built the ark. Then the day came when God told Noah and his sons and their wives to enter into the ark for their own safety and preservation. God also told Noah to take two of every kind of bird and animal to preserve God's creation (v. 19).

Evidently others had the opportunity to enter the ark so they would be safe when the floods came because the Bible calls Noah a *preacher* of righteousness (2 Peter 2:5). However, the wicked people of that generation didn't listen or take advantage of the opportunity.

> **GENESIS 6:13,14,16**
> **13 And God said unto Noah, The end of all flesh is come before me; for the earth is filled with violence through them; and, behold, I will destroy them with the earth.**
> **14 MAKE THEE AN ARK of gopher wood; rooms shalt thou make in the ark, and shalt pitch it within and without with pitch. . . .**
> **16 A window shalt thou make to the ark, and in a cubit shalt thou finish it above; and THE DOOR OF THE ARK shalt thou set in the side thereof; with lower, second, and third stories shalt thou make it.**

Notice something that the Bible says in this passage. God specifically told Noah to build the ark with a door on it. But I want you to notice something in the next verse. Noah didn't shut the door of the ark himself; he couldn't. The Bible said that it was the Lord who shut the door of the ark on Noah and his family. Although the door was a door of salvation to Noah and his family, the door also represented a door of judgment to those without or to those outside the ark.

GENESIS 7:16
16 And they that went in, went in male and female of all flesh, as God had commanded him: AND THE LORD SHUT HIM IN.

The Lord shut the door on Noah and his family to protect them from the wrath that was coming. By shutting the door, God shut out the wrath from these eight souls who were saved by water (1 Peter 3:20).

You see, there finally came a time when the Lord shut the door! Noah didn't shut it!

Well, human nature hasn't changed a bit since the time of the flood. In times of trouble, men will do all they can to preserve their own lives to save themselves. That's why I'm well satisfied that many of those wicked people tried to get into that ark after God had already shut the door. But the doors that God shuts, no man can open.

When the rain descended and the flood came, that old ark began to float! The water kept rising until it was above the housetops and the treetops. Probably many of Noah's relatives, friends, and neighbors came swimming around that old ark crying out, "Noah, let us in! Noah, let us in!"

But, you see, it was too late. Noah couldn't open the door for them because he hadn't shut it. God had shut the door. The same door that shut Noah and his family *in*, shut *out* those wicked folks. They should have entered the ark of safety when Noah preached and gave them the opportunity (2 Peter 2:5).

The shutting of these doors and the inability of men to open doors once it's too late remind me of another door or opening, and that is the gates of hell.

Gates of Hell Will Be Eternally Shut

Jesus told believers that the gates of hell shall not prevail against the Church (Matt. 16:18). In other words, Satan's kingdom of darkness won't be able to overcome the Church of the Lord Jesus Christ. And one day the literal gates of hell themselves shall be finally closed, eternally shutting in the ungodly and wicked who refused to accept the salvation that Jesus provided for them.

But God did not create hell for people; He created it for the devil and his demons (Matt. 25:41). God doesn't send any person to hell. A person sends himself to hell by his own sin of rejecting the Lord Jesus Christ as His Savior.

God does not shut the doors of salvation to keep people from receiving Jesus. He gives people a choice; they are the only ones who can shut the door of salvation on themselves. But one day, the gates of hell will be shut eternally, and those who rejected Jesus Christ will be forever lost.

Also, one day the doors of Heaven will be shut against the workers of iniquity. The Bible tells us this in Revelation 21:27. It says, ". . . *there shall in no wise enter into it* [Heaven] *any thing that defileth, neither whatsoever worketh abomination, or maketh a lie. . . ."*

We can see this more clearly in *The Amplified Bible.*

> **REVELATION 21:27 (*Amplified*)**
> **27 But nothing that defiles or profanes or is unwashed shall ever enter it [Heaven], nor any one who commits abominations — that is, unclean, detestable, morally repugnant things — or practices falsehood, but only those whose names are recorded in the Lamb's Book of Life.**

Dear friend, just the thought of a soul being eternally separated from God and from his loved ones ought to be enough to set us on the run to win the lost.

Also, just the thought of being eternally separated from God ought to be enough to encourage every person who isn't sure if he is saved to accept Jesus and get his heart right with God.

Sometimes people say, "Well, I'll just take a chance on it. I'm basically a good person. I go to church, so I *think* I'll go to Heaven when I die."

But if you know Jesus, you don't have to take a chance on your salvation! You don't have to wonder in your heart whether or not you will make Heaven! When you accept Jesus into your heart as your Lord and Savior, you can know for sure that you will go to Heaven when you die!

As long as you stay in Christ, your salvation is not based on chance — it is based on certainty! Therefore, if you've been a backslider — if you haven't been walking with God — you need to get back into fellowship with Him.

Don't wait until it is too late because there is going to be a great homegoing one day. One day believers are going home to spend eternity with Jesus, and you don't want to miss it.

The Bible also says there will be weeping and gnashing of teeth for those who miss the opportunity to go to Heaven (Matt. 13:42,50; 25:30). May no one reading this miss the opportunity to make Heaven their home!

In the natural realm, neglected opportunities bring regrets. In the spiritual realm, how much more do neglected opportunities bring regret! Missing salvation and Heaven and spending eternity in hell brings a regret that lasts forever.

In the natural realm, I've seen men who let an opportunity slip by them actually become weak and die premature. Their lives were changed and ruined; their very hearts seemed to be broken. Think how much more grief and torment it would be to miss the opportunity to get saved and go to Heaven!

Lost Opportunity Brings Eternal Regret

I remember that in my hometown, there was a young man who was just a little older than I was who got married and had children. When his children got older, they began to go to church.

Sometimes this man would come to some of my services. He'd get under conviction and just cry like a baby. Tears would actually run off his face and fall on the floor. He'd shake under the convicting power of the Holy Spirit just like he was having a chill, but I couldn't get him to give his heart to God.

Yet Jesus had opened wide the door of salvation to him! I talked to this man personally about his salvation many times.

In fact, one night he and I walked a mile or two home from a service, and I talked to him about his salvation. I knew he needed to get right with God; he was a sinner, living in immorality. He was married and fooling around with other women.

I said to him, "You know, you are raising a family now. You've got children to think of. For the sake of your family as well as for your own sake, get them in church and live for God yourself." But somehow or another, I couldn't get through to him. He would never accept Jesus and get saved.

The years came and went. Finally, I left the pastoral ministry and went out into the field ministry, traveling and teaching. One time I was holding a meeting way out in west Texas. God spoke to me in the nighttime about this man.

I was praying between three and four o'clock in the morning around the altar of the church where I was holding a revival. I've always done a lot of praying in the nighttime.

God spoke to me and told me to go back to my hometown to talk to this man one more time about accepting his salvation. Think of that! God sent me more than three hundred miles all the way from west Texas to my hometown in east Texas to talk to one lost soul!

This man had left his wife and five children and had run off with another woman. God sent me to him and told me exactly what to say to him. I traced him down and finally found him and began talking to him about accepting Jesus. Every time I opened my mouth and talked about him giving his heart to the Lord, he'd jump just like I'd hit him with a whip.

I mean, he literally shook from the top of his head to the soles of his feet. And he cried just like someone who had lost a loved one. I've never seen a grown man sob and shake and cry like he did. I finally got my message delivered to him — that he needed to get his heart right with God and get saved.

He said, "Ken, I know you are right. I know you love me. I know everything you've said is so. I know what I ought to do, but I'm not going to do it.

"I know I ought to be saved. I know I ought to give my life to Jesus. I know I ought to live right. I know what's right. But I'm not going to do it. I'm not going to do it!" and he turned and walked off and left me just sitting there.

Well, I went back to west Texas to preach. I was greatly concerned about him though. So again early in the morning about four o'clock, I was lying on the platform of the church sanctuary praying for him.

All of a sudden, the word of the Lord came to me, saying, "Leave him alone. Don't pray for him. Don't ever pray another prayer for him."

I said, "Oh, dear God!" I got up off the floor and cried, "Oh, Lord! That must not be right. Surely I should pray for him!"

The Lord said, "Did you ever read in My Word in the Old Testament where I said concerning Ephraim, 'Leave Ephraim alone. Leave him alone! He's joined to his idols'?"

> **HOSEA 4:17**
> **17 Ephraim is joined to idols: LET HIM ALONE.**

God said that! In other words, God finally closed the door on Ephraim. God was telling one of His prophets, "Don't prophesy to him anymore. Leave him alone. He's joined to his idols. Don't ever pray for Ephraim again."

Oh, that's a sad commentary! Lost opportunities bring regret. God gave this man many opportunities to accept his salvation through Jesus Christ, but the man would never receive Jesus. He absolutely refused to give his heart to God.

But that is not the end of the story about this man. This fellow had a beautiful, blond-headed little boy. The child was smart, and he loved to go to church. He loved the Lord. This little boy was saved even as a little child.

But one day, something happened to him. His teacher wrote a note to his mother and said, "Come talk to me." Something had happened to the child's mind. Then his mother began to watch him. In the wintertime, this little child would stand in front of an open stove; his clothes would catch on fire because he had no feeling in his body at all.

His mother took him to the doctors, but they couldn't find out what was wrong with him. Finally his mind was completely gone. They didn't have any place to put a child like that in those days. The state wouldn't keep him, so finally they put him in a home for mentally-handicapped children. I was attending a convention near the town where the child was institutionalized, so I said to my wife, "Let's go out there and see if we can visit that child. He should be fifteen or sixteen years old by now."

So my wife and I visited the home where the boy lived. In fact, we talked to the doctor who was the head of the institution. He sent for this boy, but he told us, "Now you'll be shocked when you see him. When you last saw him, he was probably about nine or ten years old. Is that right?"

I said, "Yes, that's right."

He said, "You see, instead of progressing, he has regressed, so he's not as big as he used to be. He's not even as big as a six-year-old child. Now he's about the size of a five-year-old child."

When the attendant finally brought the child in to see us, I wouldn't have recognized him except that the doctor had described him to me. I was shocked. I had known the child personally, so I tried to talk to him and get through to him to see if he'd know me, but he didn't. It was pitiful to see him in that condition.

This doctor asked, "Do you know this boy's family?"

"Yes," I said.

"Are you planning on seeing them?" the doctor asked.

"Yes. They live in my hometown, and my wife and I are going there after we attend a convention."

Then the doctor said, "Well, tell them that if they want to see him alive, they'd better come over to see him now. He'll not be alive much longer. He could be gone within a month or six weeks."

After the convention, my wife and I went to my home town to visit my relatives. We were driving down the street, and I saw this boy's daddy. He was only thirty-seven years old at the time, but he was living in sin, his body was eaten up with disease, and he looked like an old man.

When he got close enough to us, my wife said, "Isn't that So-and-so?"

I looked at him and said, "Yes, I believe it is."

We stood there and watched this man walk down the street toward us. We could tell by the way he was acting that he could hardly see, but when he finally got up close to us, he recognized me. Unashamedly right out on the main street in the courthouse square, he hollered out, "Ken! Oh, Ken!"

He asked me, "Do you know where my boy is? Do you know where my boy is?"

I said, "Yes, I know where he is." And I told him what the doctor had told me.

He began to cry and moan right out there on the street in broad daylight. "Oh! Oh! Isn't there something I can do to help my boy?"

I said, "No, no. There is nothing you can do now. You could have done something before. I talked to you many times about repenting and getting right with the Lord, but you said no. Over and over again you refused to give your heart to the Lord and get saved."

You talk about hell! You talk about eternal torment! That man kept rejecting Jesus Christ, and finally the door of salvation closed on him. But *he* closed the door of salvation on himself by refusing to accept Jesus Christ as his Savior.

Whatever happened to him? I heard that he died cursing God. The door of salvation closed on him because he rejected Jesus. Neglected opportunities bring regret. And when the lost opportunity is salvation, the regret lasts forever.

Jesus Shuts the Door of Opportunity

The Bible teaches us that one of the doors Jesus shuts is the door of opportunity. For example, the parable of the ten virgins is a parable about lost opportunity. In this parable, the Kingdom of God is likened to a marriage. Ten virgins are going forth to meet Jesus, the Bridegroom.

The cry went out: ". . . *Behold, the bridegroom cometh; go ye out to meet him*" (Matt. 25:6). Each one of the ten virgins had the same opportunity. Each of them had a lamp to burn oil. Each one of them was waiting in anticipation for the Bridegroom. They were each called to go out to meet the Bridegroom.

But the Bible says that five of the virgins were ready; they had extra oil so they could go out and meet the Bridegroom. Five of the virgins didn't bother to get extra oil for their lamps, so they were not prepared to meet Him when He came.

The cry came at midnight: "Behold, the Bridegroom cometh." All the virgins arose to trim their lamps, but the five foolish virgins didn't have enough oil for their lamps. They went to buy oil, but when they got back, the Bible said that the door was shut.

MATTHEW 25:6-13

6   And at midnight there was a cry made, BEHOLD, THE BRIDEGROOM COMETH; go ye out to meet him.

7   Then all those virgins arose, and trimmed their lamps.

8   And the foolish said unto the wise, Give us of your oil; for our lamps are gone out.

9   But the wise answered, saying, Not so; lest there be not enough for us and you: but go ye rather to them that sell, and buy for yourselves.

10 And while they went to buy, the bridegroom came; and they that were ready went in with him to the marriage: and THE DOOR WAS SHUT.

11 Afterward came also the other virgins, saying, Lord, Lord, OPEN TO US.

12 But he answered and said, Verily I say unto you, I know you not.

13 Watch therefore, for ye know neither the day nor the hour wherein the Son of man cometh.

Remember that a parable is like a story — it has one central truth or moral to teach us.

In any parable, find out the one central truth or thought that Jesus wants to get over to us. Then don't add to it or build anything on it.

Therefore, what is the moral of this parable about the ten virgins? Jesus is telling us, the Church, to be prepared like a bride is prepared for the coming of the bridegroom. Be ready! If you aren't ready, get ready. Otherwise, the door of opportunity will be shut. Don't try to build anything else on that one central thought.

How do you get ready? If you've never been born again, get saved. Accept Jesus into your heart so you can be born again. Then once you are saved, stay ready. Walk in fellowship with God. Walk in the light of His Word.

These five virgins who were ready went in, and the door was shut. In the meantime, the other five went to get oil for their vessels, but it was too late. The door had been shut.

The thought here is that the door of opportunity will one day be closed. Now you can preach this to sinners because this is true. They can sin away their day of grace. The door of opportunity to be saved will one day be closed, for the door of salvation will finally one day be shut.

Once Jesus shuts the door, no man can open it. So be ready to meet Jesus because the door of opportunity will not always be open.

The same thing is true in life. If a door of opportunity is opened, but you don't enter in through that door, it will eventually be closed to you.

Even in the natural, we regret it when doors of opportunity close in our lives, don't we? Neglected opportunities bring regret.

For example, many people have had an opportunity to do certain things in life, but they flubbed their opportunity. Some never had another chance, and they lived to regret it for the rest of their lives.

My friend, how much more will neglected spiritual opportunities bring regret, not only in this life, but throughout all of eternity!

In the Bible, we can see examples of people who neglected their opportunities.

For example, in the days of the New Testament, God was pouring out His Spirit on the Early Church. Right in the midst of that wonderful outpouring were two people by the name of Ananias and Sapphira. They were right in the middle of what God was doing, yet they missed out on the move of God. They missed their opportunity!

It wasn't God's fault that Ananias and Sapphira missed their opportunity. They missed it through sin and wrongdoing (Acts 5:1-10). But this shows us an important truth.

You can be right in the midst of what God is doing and miss the whole thing. How can that be possible? Because sin will always cause you to miss the mark. Also, just getting too busy in the affairs of life and not spending enough time with God can cause you to miss what God wants to do in your life.

You've got to have your heart and mind open to God so you know what He has planned for you. If you've got your mind closed and your spiritual ears shut, you can miss God's opportunities for you. It's better to keep your mouth shut and your ears open!

You see, the Bible says, ". . . *let every man be swift to hear, slow to speak, slow to wrath*" (James 1:19). Most Christians practice that in reverse. They are quick to wrath and quick to talk, but slow to hear. That's not what God said. He said to be swift to *hear* and slow to *speak*.

I found out when I was just a teenager that generally the less you talk, the less you have to repent of. And I found out early in life that you can learn a whole lot more by listening than you can by talking.

So keep your spiritual ears open to God and His Word! Don't let your doors of opportunities close on you — enter into everything that God has provided for you!

Move with God while doors of opportunities are open. And if you are not ready to meet Jesus, then while the door of opportunity is still open, get yourself ready! Walk in close fellowship with Him.

Each one of us has the same open door of opportunity so we can prepare ourselves to be ready to meet Jesus! But the day will come when we won't have time to get ready. It will be too late; the door of opportunity will already be shut.

The Bible teaches that the door of opportunity will one day be closed. For example, if a person keeps rejecting the salvation that Jesus has already provided for him, one day the gates of hell will clang shut behind him, and it will be too late for that poor lost soul.

Don't Miss Your Doors of Opportunity

Jesus Himself gives us the account in the most minute detail of a man who suffered a lost opportunity that will last for the rest of eternity. In Luke 16, Jesus said that there was a certain rich man who waited until it was too late. Finally, the doors of opportunity were closed on him.

> **LUKE 16:19-26**
> **19 There was a certain rich man, which was clothed in purple and fine linen, and fared sumptuously every day:**
> **20 And there was a certain beggar named Lazarus, which was laid at his gate, full of sores,**
> **21 And desiring to be fed with the crumbs which fell from the rich man's table: moreover the dogs came and licked his sores.**
> **22 And it came to pass, that the beggar died, and was carried by the angels into Abraham's bosom: the rich man also died, and was buried;**
> **23 And IN HELL HE LIFT UP HIS EYES, BEING IN TORMENTS, and seeth Abraham afar off, and Lazarus in his bosom.**
> **24 And he cried and said, Father Abraham, have mercy on me, and send Lazarus, that he may dip the tip of his finger in water, and cool my tongue; FOR I AM TORMENTED IN THIS FLAME.**
> **25 But Abraham said, Son, remember that thou in thy lifetime receivedst thy good things, and likewise Lazarus evil things: but now HE IS COMFORTED, and THOU ART TORMENTED.**

26 And beside all this, between us and you THERE IS A GREAT GULF FIXED: so that they which would pass from hence to you cannot; neither can they pass to us, that would come from thence.

Actually, this is not a parable because Jesus said, *"a certain rich man"* and *"a certain beggar named Lazarus"* (vv. 19,20). Evidently, He had actual people in mind when He said that.

In this account, Jesus describes the torments of hell, including the fires of hell that tormented this rich man. The rich man said, *". . . I am tormented in this flame."* So from this account, we know that there are fires of hell that torment lost souls for eternity.

Jesus also explained that there was "a great gulf fixed," so that those in hell could not escape. Hell is the place of torments. Those who were in hell could not cross over and enter into Abraham's Bosom or paradise.

Who fixed that gulf? God did. God shut the door, so to speak, *". . . so that they which would pass from hence to you cannot; neither can they pass to us, that would come from thence"* (v .26).

In other words, God shut the door so those in the place of torments could not cross over into Abraham's Bosom. And those in Abraham's Bosom — the place of comfort — could not cross over into hell.

You see, my friend, once a sinner rejects Jesus and the gates of hell clang shut on his poor lost soul, it is too late. That means you are not going to be able to pray someone out of hell into paradise. Once those gates of hell have clanged shut on someone, he is forever lost.

That ought to be enough to make a soulwinner out of every one of us! There is a Heaven to gain and a hell to shun. We are all going to leave this earth one of these days, and we are the ones who choose our eternal abode.

And whether we like it or not, we are either going by the route of death or we are going by the Rapture of the Church when Jesus comes and the trumpet of God is sounded (1 Cor. 15:52; 1 Thess. 4:16).

Those who are saved are going to depart to be with Christ. Those who are not in Christ are going down into that dark place of torments. The choice is up to each person.

The Bible says, *". . . choose you this day whom ye will serve . . ."* (Joshua 24:15). Therefore, the choice is yours.

The door of opportunity is open for each person to choose his own destiny. Each person has the power to choose the place of his eternal abode. He can choose Heaven or hell.

DEUTERONOMY 30:19
19 I call heaven and earth to record this day against you, that I have set before you life and death, blessing and cursing: therefore [you] choose life, that both thou and thy seed may live.

God Himself said, *"You* choose between life and death, blessing and cursing. *You* make the choice." You see, if a person refuses to be saved by accepting Jesus as his Savior, the day will eventually come when the door of salvation will be shut forever.

Many people in this life are full of frivolity and foolishness about the things of God. They are ready to poke fun at those who believe the Bible. Some would even tell us that hell is outdated and outmoded and that it doesn't exist. But I want to tell you that the Lord Jesus Christ taught that Hell is real and Heaven is real (Matt. 10:28; 18:3).

There is a hell to shun and a Heaven to gain! Oh, yes, in the midst of the physical vigor and strength of this life, it is easy to make fun of the things of God. It is easy to be frivolous and foolish and not take eternal things seriously.

But it is another story when you come to the end of life's journey and have to cross over to the other side and enter into that dark place to dwell in an eternal hell without God.

I remember when I was lying on the bed of sickness, a lady used to come to visit my grandma. I was living with my grandparents at the time. One evening Granny and this other woman were visiting in my room. This woman was about sixty years of age at the time.

Now the subject of God or His Word was one thing you didn't talk about when this woman was in the room. She was adverse to those things. In fact, she was so violently opposed to the things of God, that she would fly into a rage when God, the Bible, or church were mentioned. That day, some way or another, the conversation worked around to the things of God. I hadn't said a word, because I didn't want to get her started on one of her tirades. I knew she would just start ranting and raving if you talked about God.

But somehow or another we touched on the subject of the Bible, and she started ranting, "Oh, there's nothing to the Bible! It's just a hoax that's been propagated by man.

"I'll tell you! We'd be better off here in America if they would just bomb every church and kill every preacher. Preachers are just out for money, and they tell big tales and make out like there is a hell just to scare people so they can get their money!"

She ranted and raved, "Why, when you die, you're just dead like a dog, and that's the end of it!"

Momma knew this kind of talk would upset me because I was so sick anyway, so she got this woman off on another subject. This woman was all right until she would get on that one subject, and then she would just get to raving.

Twelve years later, my wife and I were out in evangelistic work. It was during World War II, and we stopped by my hometown to visit some of our relatives.

Momma said to me, "Son, go by and visit (and she called this woman's name). Pay our respects to her family because she is right at the point of death." I agreed to go.

Soon after that my wife and I traveled to this city where this woman lived. We rang the doorbell, and this woman's daughter came to the door. I recognized her right away even though it had been all those years since I'd seen her.

I told her who I was, and she said, "Oh, yes, you're Lilly's boy, the one who became a preacher."

I said, "Yes, that's me," and I introduced my wife to her.

She shook hands with us, and then she said, "Ken, Momma's not doing well. The doctor just left. Momma is in a deep coma, and the doctor said she will never regain consciousness; she'll just die.

"You know how Momma felt about the church and about God and the Bible. But please see if you can talk to her before she dies."

I agreed to try to talk to her, and the daughter led my wife and I across the living room into a bedroom where this woman lay deep in a coma.

As we went into the bedroom, we saw this woman, now about seventy-two years old lying on a bed. Her mouth was open, and her eyes were set in death — fixed wide open and just as glassy as marbles. You could hear the death rattle in her throat.

Her daughter said to her, "Momma!" There was no answer, just the labored breathing and that rattle in her throat. She called again louder, "Momma!" Again, there was no answer. Those eyes never flickered, that mouth never moved, that death rattle never stopped in her throat.

The daughter called again louder, "Momma!" then she shook her to try to get her to respond. Those eyes never moved, but somewhere from down inside her, a voice came out from way down deep inside her throat somewhere, "Yeah."

The daughter said again, "Momma, do you know me?"

"Yeah, it's my baby. It's my baby." This daughter was the only living child she had left.

The daughter said, "Momma, do you remember Lilly and her son, Ken, who was on the bed of sickness? He's the one who became a preacher."

When she said that, it snapped that old woman out of that stupor. Her eyes never changed; they were still wide open and looked like marbles. They never moved, but suddenly, she rose up, and said, "Ken! Ken! Ken! Where are you?" She couldn't see. She said, "Give me your hand!"

I took her hand in mine, and she said, "Oh, Ken! You're a preacher. Tell me there is no hell! Tell me when I die, I'm dead like a dog. Oh, it's so dark, and I'm afraid to go. I'm afraid to go! I'm so afraid to go." And before I could say one word to her, she fell back on the pillow and died without God.

Now all these many years later — almost fifty years later — as we go about our daily lives, she is in that region of darkness and of the damned, crying for light — crying for God.

Today as we quench our thirst with a cold glass of water, for all these many years she has been crying out, "Water! Water!"

Some people argue and fuss about whether or not there is a literal fire in hell. They say, "Well, I'm not convinced about the fire and all the eternal punishment of hell."

But I believe there is a literal fire in hell and eternal torment because the Bible says so (Rev. 20:14).

Jesus Himself talked about a literal fire in hell that is eternal (Matt. 5:22;13:42; Mark 9:43-47).

And in this passage we just read about the rich man and Lazarus in Luke 16:24, Jesus said there was fire in hell. Jesus related that the rich man said, ". . . *I am tormented in this flame.*"

But in another sense, whether there is a fire in hell or not is unimportant. There will be enough torment in hell for a lost soul to spend an eternity regretting the fact that he missed Heaven and that hell is his eternal abode.

The punishment of eternal separation from God and the regret and the conscious knowing that he'd missed Heaven — would be punishment enough.

Perhaps there is someone reading this who is not saved. My friend, if you are unsaved, and if you don't accept Jesus, you will be lost. And throughout eternity you are going to cry out and regret that you didn't give your heart to the Lord.

The Bible says there will be weeping, wailing, and gnashing of teeth in hell (Matt. 25:30). In eternity it will be a torment to the unsaved that Jesus wanted to save them, but they wouldn't let Him.

I pray that if you have never walked through the door of salvation Jesus Christ has provided for you, you would accept the salvation that He is so freely offering for you.

If you've never been born again, you can experience the new birth. You need to know the Lord Jesus Christ personally, because there is a Heaven to gain and a hell to shun!

And if you are like the prodigal son, and were once in the Father's house but left and went out into the practice of sin and wrongdoing, you need to know you can come back home. You can get back into fellowship with God. You can say, "Father, I have sinned against You. Please forgive me" (Luke 15:11-32).

So walk through the door of salvation that the Lord Jesus Christ has prepared for you and begin enjoying the benefits that salvation provides.

And if you are already saved because you have walked through that door of salvation, you can experience everything that God has for you that is included in your salvation — healing, health, deliverance, soundness, and wholeness!

Chapter 3
Jesus Opens the Door
Of the Heart

Another door the Lord opens for us is the door of the heart. We can see an example of that in Acts 16. You remember that Paul and his company had attempted to go into Bithynia. But the Scripture says that the Spirit forbade them (Acts 16:7).

Then in a vision in the nighttime, a man stood before Paul and said, ". . . *Come over into Macedonia, and help us*" (Acts 16:9). Therefore, the disciples believed that God was leading them to go in to Macedonia.

At that time, the gospel had only been preached right around that vicinity, which today we call Asia Minor. It had not spread into the whole region of Asia, nor had it spread into Europe.

So Paul and his company went into the continent of Europe to Macedonia and Philippi. In Philippi on the Sabbath day, the apostles were at the riverside where the people were holding a prayer meeting. The Bible talks about one woman in particular whose *heart* the Lord opened to receive the gospel.

The Word Opens People's Hearts

We can learn something from this passage about how God opens people's hearts to receive His Word.

> **ACTS 16:13,14**
> 13 And on the sabbath we went out of the city by a river side, where prayer was wont to be made; and we sat down, and spake unto the women which resorted thither.
> 14 And A CERTAIN WOMAN named Lydia, a seller of purple, of the city of Thyatira, which worshipped God, heard us: WHOSE HEART THE LORD OPENED, that she attended unto the things which were spoken of Paul.

I want you to notice that phrase, *". . . a certain woman . . . whose heart the Lord opened. . . ."* How does God open people's hearts?

God opens people's hearts with His Word. When the Word is preached, it will open people's hearts if they will listen to it and be receptive to it. But if they reject the truth of the Word, it won't have free course in their hearts.

And, for example, if people continually reject the truth of the Word about salvation, they will go into eternal darkness when they die.

> **MARK 16:15,16**
> 15 And he said unto them, Go ye into all the world, and PREACH THE GOSPEL [the Word] TO EVERY CREATURE.
> 16 He that BELIEVETH and is baptized shall be saved; but he that BELIEVETH NOT shall be damned.

Paul did what this verse said — he *preached* the Word of God to these folks so they could *believe* the truth of the gospel. The people who listened that day had the choice to accept or reject the Word that Paul preached.

Maybe others were gathered at the riverside that day with Lydia who did not allow the Word to have free course in their minds and hearts. We don't know for sure because the Bible doesn't comment on it.

We don't know how many people were there, but we do know that Lydia chose to allow the Word entrance into her heart. Lydia's heart was opened because she had an open *mind* to what she heard.

You see, we each have a will of our own. We can choose to close the door of our heart or to open it.

Therefore, in one sense the mind is the door to the heart. This is exactly what the Bible says. When your mind is *not* open to the truth of God's Word, your heart is hindered from receiving.

2 CORINTHIANS 4:4
4 In whom the god of this world HATH BLINDED THE MINDS of them which BELIEVE NOT, lest the light of the glorious gospel of Christ, who is the image of God, should shine unto them.

2 CORINTHIANS 3:14,15
14 But THEIR MINDS WERE BLINDED: for until this day remaineth the same veil untaken away in the reading of the old testament; which veil is done away in Christ.
15 But even unto this day, when Moses is read, the veil is upon their HEART.

You see, the Bible refers to the relationship between the mind and the heart. When a person's mind is closed, it is hard for him to believe the truth of God's Word in his heart.

So on the one hand, it was the Word that opened the door of Lydia's heart. But on the other hand, she had to accept the Word that was preached. Lydia had to have a mind and heart receptive to the Word that was preached. Then by an act of her will, she had to accept the Lord Jesus Christ into her heart.

You see, Jesus Himself declared that He stands at the door of a person's heart. He said, *"Behold, I STAND AT THE DOOR, and KNOCK: if any man HEAR MY VOICE, and OPEN THE DOOR, I will come in to him, and will sup with him, and he with me"* (Rev. 3:20).

It is Jesus' responsibility to stand at the door of each man's heart and do the knocking. Jesus always fulfills His responsibility to open a person's heart. He stands at the door of the heart and knocks. Then the person must yield and open the door to Jesus and His Word.

Therefore, it's not just God's Word working alone that opens a person's heart. Man works in cooperation with God by yielding to God's Word.

Jesus stands at the door of a person's heart, but then a person has to open his *mind* to hear what Jesus has to say — His Word.

But it is each person's responsibility whether or not he will respond and open the door of his heart to receive Jesus. If a person will respond to Jesus, Jesus will come and live inside his heart and unveil the Word to him.

That's what happened with this woman, Lydia. God didn't just single her out and say, "I'm going to open this woman's heart and close everyone else's heart."

Jesus stood at the door of her heart and knocked as Paul preached the Word. But then Lydia did something about it! She received the truth of the Word.

If people were there that day who did *not* accept the truth of the gospel, they closed their own hearts by closing their *minds* to the gospel — they chose not to hear and receive the Word.

But God was able to open this woman's heart with the Word because her mind was opened to the truth Paul preached, and she yielded to the Word that was preached.

So you can see that if the Word of God can find entrance into people's hearts, they can be saved and helped.

God Responds to Open Hearts

There is also a side thought here that is very interesting. Some folks are opposed to women having anything to do with preaching the gospel. Some think that men are supposed to do it all, and that women should just be in the background when it comes to the gospel.

But did you ever stop to think that the first person whose heart the Lord opened on the continent of Europe was this woman, Lydia. And after Lydia was saved, the Bible says that the disciples fellowshipped with Lydia and her household.

ACTS 16:15
**15 And when she was baptized, and her house-
hold, she besought us, saying, If ye have judged me
to be faithful to the Lord, come into my house, and
abide there. And she constrained us.**

And, of course, because of the salvations that
occurred at Philippi, a church was established in that
city. Then others opened their hearts to the truth of the
gospel as well. In fact, we have a letter — the Book of
Philippians — written by Paul to the Body of Christ in
that area.

Also, Jesus sent a woman to be the first one to tell
about His resurrection. God sent an angel to tell Mary,
*". . . go quickly, and tell his disciples that he is risen
from the dead . . ."* (Matt. 28:7). Therefore, Mary was
the first preacher of the good news of Jesus' resurrection to the disciples.

Well, thank God for open, receptive hearts to God's
precious holy Word. Thank God for women whose
hearts are open to the Word! God will use anyone whose
heart is open to the truth of the gospel.

Why was Lydia's heart open and other people's
hearts were *not* open or receptive? It's like someone once
said, "The same sun that melts wax will harden clay."

In other words, the same gospel that will open some
people's hearts will shut the hearts of others because
they refuse to accept the truth they are hearing. It is
not God's fault that some people persist in keeping their
minds and hearts closed to the truth they hear any
more than it is the sun's fault for melting wax or hardening clay.

Therefore, is all the responsibility on God to open people's hearts? No. That's exactly what the Bible is talking about in Revelation 3:20. Jesus stands at the door of each man's heart and knocks. The Bible says, "... *whosoever will, let him take the water of life freely*" (Rev. 22:17).

Each person must decide for himself what he is going to do about accepting Jesus. First, each person has the responsibility to *hear* God's voice (Rev. 3:20). Second, he must *open* his mind to the truth he is hearing. Finally, he must *respond* or *act on* that truth by opening the door of his heart.

Now some people try to say that God has foreordained some people to get saved, but not others. They read certain scriptures out of context and try to build doctrine on them. But you can't build doctrine on scriptures taken out of context.

For example, folks read Exodus 7:3 where God said, "I will harden Pharaoh's heart," and they accuse the Lord of hardening Pharoah's heart. They blame God for Pharoah's hard heart, saying it was impossible for Pharoah to obey God.

However, you cannot take this one verse out of context and try to build some kind of doctrine that puts all the responsibility on God for people's salvation. This verse alone taken out of context violates other Scripture that says God wants everyone to be saved.

2 PETER 3:9
9   The Lord is not slack concerning his promise, as some men count slackness; but is longsuffering

to us-ward, NOT WILLING THAT ANY SHOULD PERISH, but that ALL SHOULD COME TO REPENTANCE.

Interpreting Exodus 7:3 literally and out of context, "I will harden Pharoah's heart" does not agree with the teaching of the rest of the Bible.

Therefore, you cannot make the absolute statement that God hardened Pharoah's heart. In other words, you can't make *God* the one responsible for whether or not a person opens or closes his heart to God.

That would be tantamount to saying that by an act of His will, God made Pharoah's heart hard so it was impossible for Pharoah to obey God! That's not the just and loving God that we read about throughout the Bible!

No, you see, God gave Pharoah a choice, just as He gives every person the choice to obey Him. Pharoah could have chosen to do God's will, but *Pharoah's character determined his choice.* In other words, Pharoah chose first to harden his own heart. And the Bible specifically says in various places that Pharoah hardened his own heart (Exod. 8:15,32; 9:34; *See* also Exod. 7:22; 8:19; 13:15).

Let me go back again to the thought that the same sun that melts the wax, hardens the clay. You see, God extends His love and mercy to everyone.

But the same gospel, the same truths, and the same sunshine of God's love and mercy that melts receptive hearts and opens them to the gospel will be the very thing that others will harden their hearts against.

So is the sun to blame? Is the love of God to blame? Is God Himself to blame? No. The individual person is to blame. He *could* choose God. That's why it is so important to always be responsive to God. People need to make sure they have a mind and heart that is open to God to do His will.

Attend to God's Word

What can people do to allow the Word to find entrance into their hearts? Read Acts 16:14 again. The reason God was able to get into Lydia's heart was that *". . . she ATTENDED unto the things which were spoken of Paul."*

What does it mean when the Bible says Lydia *attended* unto the words which were spoken by Paul? The word "attended" means *to listen, to hear,* and *to heed.*

When you think about it from the natural standpoint, there was a group of people at the riverside that day who also heard the sound of Paul's voice. But all of them did not necessarily attend unto his *words.*

Lydia not only listened to the Word that Paul and Silas preached, but she heard it with an open mind and heart. Then she gave heed to what she heard.

Well, how do we use the word "attend" today? Suppose you were walking down the street and a friend saw you. The person called to you, "Say, wait a minute! I want to talk to you."

But you had an important engagement, so you answered, "Sorry, I can't talk right now. I've got something I must attend to." That just means you've got something else you must put first because it is more important.

Therefore, when the Bible says Lydia *attended* unto Paul's words, it simply means she put everything else aside and gave her full attention to what Paul was saying. She *heard* the words Paul spoke, not just with her head, but with her heart. Then she gave heed to the things she heard.

I'm convinced that if people will give their attention to the gospel and to the Word preached, God will be able to get into their hearts. That is the way He opens the door of the heart. It is through the gospel and through the Word of God that's preached. And God will open the door of every person's heart who will let Him!

God Opens the Eyes of Our Heart To Understand the Word

Many times people say, "I just can't understand the Word." But God opens the door of people's hearts so they *can* understand the Word.

For example, let's look at something that happened after the resurrection. Mary Magdalene, Joanna, and some of the women who had ministered to Jesus came to the sepulchre that first Easter morning.

They saw the empty grave, and two angels spoke to them saying, *"He is not here, but is risen . . ."* (Luke 24:6). Then the women went to tell the disciples the good news.

LUKE 24:9-11
9 . . . [the women] **returned from the sepulchre,
and told all these things unto the eleven, and to all
the rest.**
**10 It was Mary Magdalene, and Joanna, and Mary
the mother of James, and other women that were
with them, WHICH TOLD THESE THINGS UNTO
THE APOSTLES.**
**11 And THEIR WORDS SEEMED TO THEM AS
IDLE TALES, and THEY BELIEVED THEM NOT.**

The disciples didn't believe the women's report that
Jesus was alive. Their words seemed as "idle tales" to
the disciples because the eyes of their hearts were not
yet opened or enlightened by the Word. God had to open
their understanding so they could comprehend the
events that had just transpired.

You see, the Word of God is a sealed Book to many
people. That's why even some Christians say, "I just
can't understand the Bible."

We find an example of two men in the Bible who were
like that until Jesus opened the eyes of their understanding by opening the truth of the Word to them.

These two men walked along the road to Emmaus
on that first Easter day so long ago. Suddenly a stranger
came along and joined Himself with them.

He began to question them about what they were
discussing. They said to Him, "You must be a stranger
in Jerusalem. Don't you know what's been happening?"

LUKE 24:13-21,25-27,30-32
13 And, behold, two of them went that same day to

a village called Emmaus, which was from Jerusalem about threescore furlongs.

14 And they talked together of all these things which had happened.

15 And it came to pass, that, while they communed together and reasoned, Jesus himself drew near, and went with them.

16 But THEIR EYES WERE HOLDEN that they should not KNOW HIM.

17 And he said unto them, What manner of communications are these that ye have one to another, as ye walk, and are sad?

18 And the one of them . . . answering said unto him, Art thou only a stranger in Jerusalem, and hast not known the things which are come to pass there in these days?

19 And he said unto them, What things? And they said unto him, Concerning Jesus of Nazareth, which was a prophet mighty in deed and word before God and all the people:

20 And how the chief priests and our rulers delivered him to be condemned to death, and have crucified him.

21 But we trusted that it had been he which should have redeemed Israel: and beside all this, to day is the third day since these things were done. . . .

25 Then he said unto them, O fools, and SLOW OF HEART TO BELIEVE all that the prophets have spoken:

26 Ought not Christ to have suffered these things, and to enter into his glory?

27 And beginning at Moses and all the prophets, HE EXPOUNDED UNTO THEM IN ALL THE SCRIPTURES the things concerning himself. . . .

30 And it came to pass, as he [Jesus] sat at meat with them, he took bread, and blessed it, and brake, and gave to them.

**31 And THEIR EYES WERE OPENED, and THEY
KNEW HIM; and he vanished out of their sight.
32 And they said one to another, DID NOT OUR
HEART BURN WITHIN US, while he talked with
us by the way, and while HE OPENED TO US THE
SCRIPTURES?**

Jesus said that it was because the disciples were
"slow of heart" that their eyes were "holden" or spiritually closed so they didn't know Him. Well, how did
Jesus get their spiritual eyes opened or enlightened?

He unveiled the Word to them! He opened the
truths of the Word so they could see *Him* in the Scriptures. Verse 27 says, *"And beginning at Moses and all
the prophets, he expounded unto them in all the scriptures the things concerning himself."* Jesus had to open
the Scriptures to these two disciples before they could
understand the Word.

Jesus the Living Word opened and revealed the
written Word to them.

These two disciples were receptive to the Word, so it
got into their hearts. Once they received the Word
". . . their eyes were opened, and they knew him." The
Word opened their eyes so they could know Jesus!

You see, the eyes of their understanding had to be
opened before they could understand the truth of God's
Word. The Bible said that when the eyes of their hearts
were opened, *then* they knew Him (v. 31).

The psalmist of old said, *"Open thou mine eyes, that
I may behold wondrous things out of thy law"* (Ps.
119:18). I think we could paraphrase that verse like

this: "Open my eyes that I may behold wondrous truths out of thy *Word*."

The psalmist didn't mean for God to open his *physical* eyes; he was talking about his *spiritual* eyes. But Jesus does the same thing for us today. He opens the eyes of our heart so we can behold wondrous truths in God's Word!

You see, my friend, in order for this marvelous Book — the Bible — to be opened to you, you have to walk with the Master. That's the reason the Bible is a closed Book to some Christians. Many of them are not walking with Jesus in close fellowship; they are following Him afar off.

When you follow Jesus afar off, you can be "slow of heart" even as those disciples were on the road to Emmaus.

But when believers walk closely to the Lord and ask Him to open their spiritual eyes, they can begin to see truths in the Word they've never seen before.

When you become acquainted with Jesus and you know Him personally, the Bible is just different to you. When I was born again, the Bible became alive to me. I was raised in church, and before I was born again, I thought I knew Jesus.

Oh, I had joined the church like many folks. I was even baptized in water. But I went down under that water a *dry* sinner and I came up a *wet* sinner! The Bible was a closed Book to me; I couldn't understand it. The eyes of my understanding weren't enlightened or opened.

I honestly thought you weren't supposed to understand the Bible. I thought no one but the preacher could understand it. But then I was born again on April 22, 1933, at twenty minutes to eight o'clock in the south bedroom of 405 North College Street in McKinney, Texas.

Once I was born again, it was a blessing just to hold that Bible in my hands and look at it. It seemed like I was blessed for an hour just by reading the words, "Holy Bible." Just looking at the Bible, even the cover looked different because my heart was open to the truth of God's Word.

Then I looked on the inside, and I got blessed just by reading the Table of Contents. Why? Because I had become acquainted with the Author of the Book!

Praise God forevermore, He is the living Word! And when I got acquainted with Jesus, He opened the eyes of my understanding!

You see, the written Word has been given to us to unveil, unfold, and reveal the Living Word to us — Jesus Christ.

And when we fellowship with Jesus in His Word with sincere hearts, Jesus the Living Word can reveal to us the Bible — the written Word.

So as we walk in fellowship with Jesus, what can we do to get the eyes of our understanding open to behold wonders out of God's Word?

God gave us a way! The Holy Spirit through the Apostle Paul gave us Spirit-anointed, Spirit-led prayers to pray so that the eyes of our understanding could be opened — not closed — but opened to behold the truths in God's Word.

> **EPHESIANS 1:17,18**
> **17 That the God of our Lord Jesus Christ, the Father of glory, MAY GIVE UNTO YOU THE SPIRIT OF WISDOM AND REVELATION IN THE KNOWLEDGE OF HIM:**
> **18 The EYES OF YOUR UNDERSTANDING BEING ENLIGHTENED** [or opened]; **that ye may know what is the hope of his calling, and what the riches of the glory of his inheritance in the saints.**

I want you to notice something about this prayer in Ephesians 1:17 and 18. First, the Holy Spirit through Paul instructed believers to pray for the spirit of wisdom and revelation in the knowledge of Him. Then God told believers to ask God to open the eyes of their heart or understanding.

You see, once the eyes of your understanding are opened, you will know Jesus — not just know *about* Him but *know* Him in a deep and personal way.

That's exactly what happened to those disciples who walked along the road to Emmaus in Luke 24:31 that we read about. When the eyes of their understanding were opened, they knew Jesus!

We could also translate Ephesians 1:18: "I pray that the eyes of your understanding are opened to see the hope of His calling and the riches of His glory to His saints."

One translation says, "I pray that the eyes of your *spirit* may be enlightened." This is talking about the man on the inside — your spirit man — not the out-ward man, which is your body and your physical eyes.

This prayer was given by the Spirit of God for the Church at Ephesus. If it is the will of God for the saints in Ephesus to pray this prayer to enlighten or open their understanding, it must be the will of God for saints everywhere to pray this prayer too.

You can pray these prayers for yourself. We need to have the eyes of our understanding enlightened, or opened, to see and comprehend the glorious inheritance God has for us.

In the last church I pastored, I began praying these prayers in Ephesians for myself, particularly in the winter of 1947 and 1948. I just simply spent a lot of time in the Presence of God, praying these prayers. I'd always talked to God a lot, especially in the nighttime. Through the years, I have done most of my praying in the nighttime.

We form spiritual habits just like we do natural habits. When I was born again, I was on the bed of sick-ness, so I couldn't get up and go anywhere to pray. I had to pray in bed, so I would talk to God constantly in the nighttime.

I would purposely wait until everyone got into bed at night and all the lights were out. Then I'd do my praying.

Several nights I prayed nearly all night long. And nearly every night, I'd pray at least an hour or two, just talking to the Lord.

That's how I got really well-acquainted with Him. And through the years, I've just spent a lot of time in the Presence of the Lord. Then when I became a pastor, I still did a lot of my praying in the nighttime.

I'd get up and go over to pray in the church next door to the parsonage. I'd walk up and down the aisles of the church and talk to the Father. I kept my Bible in the church opened to Ephesians chapters 1 and 3.

And many times during the day as I was carrying on my other pastoral duties, I'd go into the church and just get on my knees and read these two prayers. I'd say to the Lord, "Lord, I'm praying these prayers for myself."

And when the Bible said, "I pray that the eyes of *your* understanding be enlightened or opened," I would pray, "I pray that the eyes of *my* understanding be enlightened or opened."

Then I would pray, "God, I'm praying for myself that You, the God of our Lord Jesus Christ, the Father of glory, may give unto *me* the spirit of wisdom and revelation in the knowledge of You."

I'd see to it that I went into the church at least several times a day to pray these prayers in Ephesians for myself. Some days when I wasn't as busy, I spent several hours praying these prayers for myself.

I just practiced that over a period of two or three months. Then one day I went into the church and knelt there to pray as usual. I read the Ephesians prayers and said, "Lord, I'm praying this for myself." The Lord spoke to me and said, "I'm going to take you on to revelations and visions."

First the revelations began to come. They came as a direct result of praying these prayers for myself. I don't mean strange revelations outside of God's Word; I mean revelations in line with the Word. I began to get revelation in the knowledge of Him because the eyes of my understanding were being opened to the truth of the Word (Eph. 1:16-23)!

I'd always been very studious. Many times, I'd read all night long. Not just the Bible, but other spiritual books too. I studied constantly.

But when the eyes of my understanding were opened — the eyes of my inner man — I learned spiritual truths so quickly that I said to my wife, "What in the world have I been preaching?" I learned more about the Bible and about God in six months by revelation than I'd learned in fourteen years of study and preaching put together. I quickly saw spiritual truths from the Word. I said to my wife, "I've been so stupid and ignorant, it is a wonder the deacons didn't have to come by and tell me to get in out of the rain!"

Let the Lord Bring His Will To Pass

This happened in late 1947 and on into the winter of 1948. I stayed at that church another year until February 1949. Then I went out in the field ministry. And in August 1950 Jesus again told me, "I'm going to take you on to revelations and visions."

It was several years before I experienced a vision even though Jesus had already spoken to me about this.

I didn't just jump out and try to make something happen on my own; I just let God bring His own will to pass in the matter in His own timing.

You have to be very careful about what you *think* the Lord says to you by the Holy Spirit. Don't lean to your own understanding and try to put your own interpretation on what you heard.

Also, don't try to make it come to pass yourself. Just wait, and if it is God speaking, He will bring it to pass. If He doesn't, then it either wasn't Him or else you were hopelessly unfaithful.

I think that's one problem we have today. I'm sure some folks never heard a thing from God; they just imagined the Lord told them something. Or maybe they ate too much for supper and had a wild dream or something!

Or maybe they were like the fellow down in east Texas who told this story about misinterpreting what the Lord was saying to him. I don't know if the story is true or not, but it makes a good point.

Supposedly this fellow was out plowing, but he wasn't paying attention to what he was doing, so he wasn't getting very much plowing done. He was just whiling away his time. He said he saw a sign in the sky. It said, "GP." He put his own interpretation on it and said God was telling him, "Go preach."

Actually, he came to understand later that it meant, "Go plow!" He said God was trying to get his attention so he'd get on with it and finish plowing his field instead of just fooling around wasting his time!

The point is, don't put your own interpretation on what the Lord is saying to you. That's where the problem is a lot of times. If it is God, just let God be God and allow Him to open the doors of opportunity that He has for you.

Just rest in Him, and let Him bring to pass what He's told you. Be faithful, pray, and study to prepare yourself to do His will (2 Tim. 2:15).

In my own walk with the Lord, I never try to force anything that God has told me by trying to make it come to pass myself. I've seen things in the Spirit that were years in coming to pass — some things more than fifty years — but it never bothered me a bit just to wait for God to bring it to pass.

God can open His own doors for you! Don't get in a hurry and try to open those doors by yourself. You can't get things to come to pass in your own strength anyway. Besides, God blesses you as you walk through the doors *He* opens.

When God said He would take me on to visions and revelations, the visions didn't start coming until 1950. But from 1950 through 1958, the Lord Himself appeared to me eight times.

I'm sure that never would have happened to me if I hadn't begun to pray those prayers in Ephesians, asking the Lord to open the eyes of my understanding and to give me revelation in the knowledge of Him.

How did I receive knowledge about Jesus? Of course, I've always prayed a lot in tongues. But I received knowledge about Jesus simply by praying these prayers in Ephesians word for word for myself. Jesus opened the

eyes of my heart so I could understand spiritual truths.
And He continually enlightens me as I read His Word.

You can also pray that God would open the eyes of
someone else's understanding. For example, I remember one person I knew who was saved and baptized
with the Holy Ghost and spoke with other tongues. He
needed healing in his body, and he believed in divine
healing, but he was struggling in his spiritual life. He
was having a hard time receiving his healing.

He talked to me, and I knew something about his
spiritual struggle. His lack of understanding about
healing was hindering his faith, so he couldn't get his
faith to work in the area of healing. Finally, because of
his disease, he was virtually facing death.

Well, I talked to him more than once to try to get
him to see certain biblical truths about healing; but he
just couldn't seem to grasp them.

Not too long after that, I was in a meeting in a certain city in Texas, and every day I would open my Bible
to these prayers here in Ephesians. I'd say, "Lord, I'm
praying this for So-and-so," and I'd just call his name to
the Lord. Then I'd pray these prayers for him, putting
his name in wherever it said, "you" or "your."

I prayed using this prayer in Ephesians chapter 1
that God would open the eyes of his understanding so
he could see certain truths in the Word of God. I prayed
that way for him every day for ten days.

On the tenth day, that man came to me and said,
"You know what?"

"What?" I asked.

He said, "I'm beginning to see things in the Word I've never seen before."

I never did tell him that I'd been praying that his spiritual eyes would be opened.

Praying the Ephesian prayers is a valuable way to pray for yourself, but this is a scriptural way to pray for other people too.

The reason many people don't understand the Scriptures is that they don't know Jesus. Or if they know Him, they are not walking in fellowship with Him. Therefore, the eyes of their heart aren't opened or enlightened. When their spiritual eyes are opened, they'll be able to receive knowledge of Jesus (Eph. 1:17).

Is the Word Open or Closed to You?

Friend, if we will walk in close fellowship with the Lord, He will open the Word to us. When you get acquainted with Jesus, the Bible becomes an open Book to you because you know the Author. It's not closed to you anymore.

But if you don't know Jesus the Author, it will be a closed book to you. You'll read it and say, "I didn't get a thing in the world out of that."

Normally there is a reason that the Bible is not light, but only darkness to you. If it seems to be closed to you even though you've been saved for years, then you need to get into closer fellowship with God so He can open up your spiritual eyes.

And sometimes if you are saved but the Word of God is not alive to you or open to your understanding, it could be that you are not walking in the light of the Word. In other words, you may not be walking in all the truth you know.

You see, the Bible says it is the little foxes that spoil the vines (Song of Sol. 2:15). Sometimes it is the cares of life and the little sins that creep in and get between you and God. The Bible says that sin separates you from God (Isa. 59:2). When sin separates you from God, He doesn't seem so real to you. I've learned a long time ago that when the Word was no longer illuminated to me, I'd missed it somewhere, and I needed to turn around and get back on the main road.

Have you ever been at a place in life when it seemed like you just took the wrong turn? It is just like taking a trip. You get off on the wrong road, and there is no use continuing down the wrong road — you just need to get back on the right road so you can reach your destination.

There have been a few times in life when I've just had to back up and get back on the main road. The minute I did, the Word was life and light and alive to me once again. But as long as I was on the wrong road, it was dark to me, not illuminated.

But, praise God, Jesus will open His Word to you! Jesus is the Opener! He will open the eyes of your understanding so you can behold wondrous truths in His Word!

Be a doer and a practicer of the Word, and His Word will open up to you to a greater and greater measure! Walk in the light of what you do know. When you are a doer of the Word and walk in fellowship with God, He will open up the rest of the Word to you. Whatever you need to know, He will open it up to you.

Jesus has opened the door of provision and blessing to us. As we attend to the Word and walk in close fellowship with Him, He also continues to open other doors for growth, opportunity, and service in our lives.

Chapter 4
Open Doors of Service And Utterance

Jesus opens wonderful doors of service for us! When we are obedient to walk through the doors of service the Lord opens to us, we will be amazed at the rich spiritual growth that will take place in our own personal lives. God abundantly rewards those who are obedient to do His will.

However, it is amazing to me how many believers want to do something for God, yet they are waiting until they can do something *big* for Him. But if they won't do something *little* for God, they won't ever do anything big for Him.

That's why it is so important to start out serving God wherever you are. Whatever small door He opens for you, walk through it, so He can open bigger doors of service for you.

When I first started out just as a teenager, I volunteered to do anything I could for God. If I went to someone's church, even if I wasn't a member and they needed someone to sweep the floor, I was the first one to volunteer. I'd say, "I'll do it!"

For example, once I visited a church while the pastor was trying to get someone to help him do some carpentry work in the church.

The church building was old and had never been weather-proofed on the outside. Winter was coming, so the pastor wanted to get the church ready for the bad weather.

I wasn't even a member of that church, but I volunteered to help him. The pastor and I did ninety percent of the work weather-stripping that church. I did it as unto the Lord. I wasn't working just for men. I wanted to please the Lord.

It's disappointing to see people who could really do something for God just sitting around doing nothing. For example, instead of serving God right where they are in their spiritual growth, some people who are called to the ministry will say, "Oh, I can't do *that!* Why, I'm called to be a *prophet.* I can't work in the church. God's got greater things for me than that!"

Well, in the first place, even if someone was called by God to stand in the office of the prophet, it would probably be many years before he would be mature enough ministerially to stand in that office. God doesn't put novices into ministry offices.

God wants believers to grow up spiritually before He gives them that kind of ministerial responsibility.[1]

It will save believers many pitfalls if they will understand this principle: God does not put spiritually immature Christians into offices of great responsibility.

The Spirit of God through the Apostle Paul told Timothy not even to put a novice in the office of a deacon (1 Tim. 3:6,8,10).

If the Spirit of God would say not to put a novice in the office of the deacon, then why would God put a novice in offices of even greater responsibility such as the fivefold ministry? He wouldn't!

It wouldn't be wise to do so because a novice can too easily get lifted up in pride. Satan could too easily tempt him to think more highly of himself than he ought because of his ministerial position.

No, ministries take time to develop. Besides, those who are called to the ministry probably won't end up ministering in the same office in which they begin. First God develops and matures people so they are ready for greater and greater responsibility.

The potential for ministry may be there and the calling may be there. However, believers can't step into everything God has for them overnight just because they are called of God.

This is true even in the natural. For example, a baby in its mother's arms has the potential to grow up to become a doctor, lawyer, or even the President of the United States.

But that baby can't be any of those things tomorrow or the next day. It will take time for him to grow, develop, and mature so he can handle that kind of responsibility.

Similarly, the potential is there for the full scope of a believer's ministry and service to God to come to pass, but he won't be able to step over into that immediately. It takes time to develop the full potential of a person's ministry.

But when believers are mature enough and have developed spiritually, God will begin moving them into the position He has for them. And when He is ready for it, He will open up doors of greater and greater service for them.

That is one reason believers are supposed to prepare themselves. If they don't prepare themselves, they won't be ready to move on with God. The Bible talks about this: *"Study to shew thyself approved unto God, a workman that needeth not to be ashamed, rightly dividing the word of truth"* (2 Tim. 2:15).

Many times people think they are waiting on God when really *God* is waiting on *them* to prepare themselves. One way they can prepare themselves is by studying to show themselves approved. Then when they are prepared, God will open doors for them.

What believers need to understand is that doors of service are open to every person. Therefore, find out what *your* door of service is. Ask the Lord to show you what *you* can do for *Him*.

Then wherever a door of service opens, just stick your foot in it. Whatever your hand finds to do, do it as unto the Lord. The Bible says, *"And whatsoever ye do, do it heartily, as to the Lord, and not unto men"* (Col. 3:23).

When you prove to God that you can be depended on, He will move you into the service or ministry He has for you. But if you are too proud to do the little things, God won't be able to use you in a ministry that requires great responsibility.

God Rewards Faithfulness

Sometimes people say, "God didn't call me to preach, so there's nothing I can do for Him." But there are doors of service to be opened for every person in God's Kingdom.

Whatever doors of service God opens for you, if you serve Him faithfully, you will be rewarded just as richly as those who are called to serve in a pulpit ministry.

Sometimes people think that because someone stands in the pulpit and preaches, that person will be rewarded immeasurably beyond anyone else in eternity. But that's just not so.

If you are faithful in whatever God has told you to do, you will be rewarded for your faithfulness. God doesn't reward people according to their *position*; He rewards them according to their *faithfulness* to obey Him.

You know, in the army of the Lord, not everyone is an officer. We can't all be officers any more than everyone could be officers in a natural army. There also have to be foot soldiers and others who serve in various capacities.

Even in the Old Testament, the Bible says that those who "stayed by the stuff" — those who stayed behind to guard the army's belongings — received just as much of the rewards and spoils of war as those who went out to battle. Staying by the stuff was an open door of service too.

We see an example of this principle in the Old Testament. The Amalakites came in and plundered Ziklag and kidnapped all the women and children from David's camp. David and his men mourned greatly for the loss of their families and their goods.

Finally David encouraged himself in the Lord and began to inquire of the Lord as to what to do. The Lord told David to pursue the enemy, for David and his men would surely overcome them and recover all their goods. So David gathered his men together and pursued the Amalakites.

> **1 SAMUEL 30:8-10,18-25**
> **8   And David inquired at the Lord, saying, Shall I pursue after this troop? shall I overtake them? And he answered him, Pursue: for thou shalt surely overtake them, and without fail recover all.**
> **9   So David went, he and the six hundred men that were with him, and came to the brook Besor, where THOSE THAT WERE LEFT BEHIND STAYED.**
> **10 But David pursued, he and four hundred men: FOR TWO HUNDRED ABODE BEHIND, which were so faint that they could not go over the brook Besor....**
> **18 And David recovered all that the Amalekites had carried away: and David rescued his two wives.**
> **19 And there was nothing lacking to them, neither small nor great, neither sons nor daughters, neither spoil, nor any thing that they had taken to them: David recovered all.**
> **20 And David took all the flocks and the herds, which they drave before those other cattle, and said, THIS IS DAVID'S SPOIL.**
> **21 And David came to the two hundred men, which were so faint that they could not follow David, whom they had made also TO ABIDE AT THE BROOK BESOR: and they went forth to meet David, and to meet the people that were with him:**

**and when David came near to the people, he
saluted them.
22 Then answered all the wicked men and men of
Belial, of those that went with David, and said,
BECAUSE THEY WENT NOT WITH US, WE WILL
NOT GIVE THEM OUGHT OF THE SPOIL THAT
WE HAVE RECOVERED, save to every man his
wife and his children, that they may lead them
away, and depart.
23 Then said David, Ye shall not do so, my
brethren, with that which the Lord hath given us,
who hath preserved us, and delivered the company that came against us into our hand.
24 For who will hearken unto you in this matter?
but AS HIS PART IS THAT GOETH DOWN TO THE
BATTLE, SO SHALL HIS PART BE THAT TARRI-
ETH BY THE STUFF: they shall part alike.
25 And it was so from that day forward, that HE
MADE IT A STATUTE AND AN ORDINANCE FOR
ISRAEL UNTO THIS DAY.**

You see, in David's army it was considered just as
great a service to stay behind with the supplies as it
was to go out to battle. It became an ordinance in Israel
that those who stayed behind to take care of the belongings would receive just as great a reward as those who
went out to battle.

We also see this principle today in the church. For
example, sometimes people say that missionaries pay
the greatest sacrifice in the service of the Lord because
they serve Him on foreign fields. And especially on
some foreign mission fields, missionaries do make a
tremendous sacrifice to serve God.

But sometimes obeying God on the mission field is
not any greater sacrifice than it is to obey God by "staying by the stuff" at home.

Sometimes the hardest thing to do is just stay in your own local church and community serving the Lord by entering into whatever doors of service He opens for you.

The point is that God richly blesses *obedience* — no matter where you serve Him! God will richly reward you as you walk through the door of service He has opened for *you*.

For example, over the years people have told me, "God blessed you so much because many years ago you were obedient to God and went out in the field ministry." But even though my wife stayed home with the children, her reward will be just as great as mine.

We need to realize that God will reward people for faithfully attending church and working in their local church body if that's what He's called them to do, because God rewards faithfulness.

Therefore, even though some believers just "stay by the stuff" and don't serve God on the mission field, God will reward their prayers, their financial support, and their work in their own local church body.

Some Christians say, "But there is nothing I can do." But, you know, there's some kind of service to the Lord that each one of us can do.

When some people get to Heaven and the rewards are given out, I am certain that many folks will step forward to get a certain reward, but Jesus will call someone else's name.

For example, I'm sure that there are going to be some preachers and pastors who are going to step up to receive a reward because they will think to themselves, *I know I'll receive a reward because, after all, I built that church!* Or they'll think *I did this* or *I did that.*

But I'm convinced that many times Jesus is going to call the name of some other person who worked faithfully behind the scenes, when no one knew about it but God!

Prayer Is a Service Unto the Lord

Let me give you an example of what I mean. Many people don't think about prayer as an open door of service to the Lord. But much good is wrought in the Kingdom of God by the faithful prayers of God's people.

For example, at the Pentecostal church I pastored when I first came over into the Full Gospel Movement, there was a little lady who lived in a nearby town who was about eighty-two years old. Folks called her Mother H_____.

Mother H_____ was not a member of my church, but she would visit my church quite frequently because it wasn't too far from where she lived.

I pastored in a little country town with a population of only a few hundred. Most of my congregation consisted of farmers who lived in the farming area round about, and some lived in town. Well, we'd have a fellowship meeting every Sunday, and forty to seventy people would attend.

We'd go to someone's home to have a potluck dinner and a time of fellowship. It was harvest time in the fall of the year, so we only had services on the weekends. We dismissed our Wednesday night service because people were out harvesting their crops and picking cotton.

Mother H_____ would come to these Sunday fellowship meetings that were held in someone's home. As soon as the dinner was over, Mother H_____ would fellowship a little bit, but then she would find a bedroom where she could pray.

Many of those old farm homes back in the '30s didn't have rugs on the floor; some of them didn't even have linoleum. Many of them just simply had old, rough, bare wooden floors.

Mother H_____ would ask for a magazine or a newspaper or something she could spread on the floor, and then she would get on her knees and pray the rest of the afternoon.

While the rest of us were visiting, fellowshipping, and enjoying one another's company, Mother H_____ was praying. I learned that she had lived in Dallas, Texas, and had received the baptism of the Holy Ghost way back at the turn of the century.

After Mother H_____ was filled with the Spirit, she just took it upon her heart to pray a Full Gospel church into every town and city in north Texas. She made a business of prayer. In other words, she made it her business to live a life of prayer to God.

One of the neighboring pastors didn't have a parsonage, so Mother H_____ told this pastor and his wife, "If you want to, you can live in my house." So they built a partition and made an apartment on one side of her house so the pastor and his wife could live there.

This pastor said that Mother H_____ would always arise at eight o'clock every morning and pray from eight o'clock until ten o'clock in the morning.

Then at ten o'clock she'd have something to eat and sometimes would fellowship with the pastor and his wife. But by two o'clock, she was back on her knees praying. She would pray until six o'clock in the evening.

Then maybe she would eat dinner, but by seven o'clock or so, she would be right back at prayer again and pray nearly all night long.

She did that night after night, day after day, month after month. That was her service unto the Lord. No one else knew what she was doing because she prayed in the privacy of her own home. But God saw it.

So town by town, city by city, Mother H_____ prayed until a Full Gospel church was established in every one of those towns and in every one of those cities. She prayed until it happened.

I'm well satisfied that when some of those pastors who established churches in those early days finally get up to Heaven, they are going to get all ready to step up for their reward. Then the Lord is going to call Mother H_____ forward for the reward instead. You see, Mother H_____ served the Lord by praying! Maybe she couldn't preach a sermon or go visit the sick. But there was something she could do — she could pray!

This should be a lesson to all of us, especially those who say, "But I don't know what to do to serve the Lord." God is not negligent in opening doors of service for each one of us, but many have been negligent in walking through the doors He opens!

Great and Effectual Doors of Service

I like something Paul said in First Corinthians 16:9 about open doors of service.

1 CORINTHIANS 16:9
9   For A GREAT DOOR AND EFFECTUAL IS OPENED UNTO ME, and there are many adversaries.

God opens great, effectual doors of service for us. However, commenting on this verse, we could begin this verse with the phrase, *". . . there are many adversaries."*

You see, Paul was realistic. He didn't deny the fact that there are many adversaries. Satan will always try to oppose us to keep us from going through the doors of service that the Lord has opened for us.

Sometimes people think that if you talk about the devil and you talk about problems, you are making a bad confession. But Paul wasn't making a bad confession; he was just facing facts. He was really stating a spiritual truth. Satan does try to oppose believers in their work for God.

Friend, you have to face facts. Then once you face the facts, you can take your stand in faith. But how can you stand in faith on God's Word when you don't even know what you are believing God for?

You see, many people think they are taking a stand in faith in the service of the Lord when really they are taking a stand in ignorance by denying the facts, and the devil is laughing at them the whole time. Folks need to realize that.

In other words, even though the Lord opens a door of service for you, you've still got to use some common sense and wisdom as you fulfill what the Lord has given you to do. You can't just say, "Well, I'm serving the Lord now, so He will just automatically take care of everything that concerns me."

I knew some people who did just that. For example, I was preaching at a ministry in a certain area. The people I was preaching for told me about a couple who worked in another ministry for someone else. This couple had brought their little three-year-old child to work with them, and they allowed the child to just wander all around the grounds. There was a swimming pool on the grounds, and one of the caretakers came in and told the parents, "You'd better watch your little boy or else he's going to fall into that swimming pool and drown."

Well, these people thought they were faith people and that since they were busy serving the Lord, nothing bad could happen to them. But even though God's people serve the Lord, He still expects them to use good judgment and common sense. Actually, these dear folks weren't acting in faith at all; they were just being ignorant.

Well, they were warned to watch out for their child because of that swimming pool. But they just said, "Oh, don't make a bad confession. Don't confess that over us. We'll just put the angels to work to protect our child because we're busy serving the Lord."

The next day the child drowned. You see, friend, you can't just leave children to themselves and let them do whatever they want to. It's not faith to neglect your

children and just believe God to take care of them just
because you are in the service of the Lord. Really, that's
just shirking your responsibility.

You can't just turn little children over to God and to
His angels and try to claim protection, when *you* are
failing in your responsibility as a parent to take care of
them in the first place. These people whose child
drowned thought they were standing in faith, but really
they were ignorant of the principles in God's Word. You
see, Paul believed in faith in God. He said, "Many doors
of opportunity are opened." That's faith. But he was
also realistic. He didn't ignore the fact that there is an
enemy arrayed against us. Therefore, Paul also said,
"There are *many* adversaries."

Also, notice that Paul didn't say, "There are just a
few adversaries — not enough to bother about." Or he
didn't say, "Yes, effectual doors of service are open, and
our adversary, the devil, will just let us walk right
through them unhindered."

No, Paul faced facts and told believers that the devil
will try to oppose them. But that doesn't negate the
effectual open doors of service that the Lord has provided for them. It also doesn't negate the authority that
believers have over the devil (Matt. 18:18; Luke 10:19).

You see, Paul knew how to gain the victory in every
situation! He knew believers have the victory over the
devil in Jesus' Name (Phil. 2:9,10). But on the other
hand, he did not deny the fact that there were *many*
adversaries that would try to keep Christians from
entering the doors of opportunity and service that were
opened before them.

See, Recognize, and Enter
Into Your Open Doors

To tell you the truth about the matter, there is a door of service opened before every one of us, if we will just *see* it, *recognize* its value, and *enter* into it!

You may say, "But I'm not called to preach" or "I'm not called to a pulpit ministry."

Then maybe you are called to the ministry of helps. People in the ministry of helps assist or *help* those in the fivefold ministry.

But whether or not you have a call of God to the fivefold *ministry*, if you will just look around, you will see plenty of open doors for *service* in various areas in the ministry.

I was pastor of a little country church years ago in Texas. We'd just come out of the Depression, and prices and wages were frozen because we were still operating on Depression prices.

We didn't have a regular janitor, but from time to time different people volunteered to clean the church. I'd always go over to check up to be sure they'd dusted the pews and swept the floors.

If it wasn't done right, I just did it over. Most of the time it wasn't done right, so many times, I'd just wind up cleaning the church myself.

Well, one of the young men of my church had gone out into the ministry, and he was the pastor of a little country church about thirty miles away. I'd promised him that I would hold a meeting for him, so I held a revival in his church. We had a service every night, from Monday night through Saturday night.

After the Saturday night service, I drove back home so I could preach the next morning in my own church. We didn't have freeways back then, just two-lane roads, and people didn't travel as fast in those days as they do now. And after the service we had some refreshments and fellowship, so I didn't get home until late.

I remember driving along thinking, *I hope they've cleaned the church. If they didn't, I'm going to have to get up early in the morning or else do it before I go to bed tonight so it will be clean for the Sunday morning service.* We had volunteers who cleaned the church, but sometimes folks would say they were going to clean it but didn't follow through and do it.

So when I got to the parsonage, the first thing I did was to go over to the church and turn on the lights. The church was just spick and span. It was unusually clean; it had never looked that immaculate before. So I rejoiced and went on my way.

The next morning after the Sunday morning service, a brother came up to me just beaming and said, "Well, what do you think of it?"

He was just so thrilled, you would have thought he had just been elected as the pastor of the church or that he'd just been promoted to some high office or something.

"Think about what?" I asked.

"The church! Didn't you notice how clean it was?" he said just beaming.

"Yes," I said. "That is the best job that's ever been done on it."

When I said that, the man just began to weep. He said, "Brother Hagin, I'm a member of this church. I never went to school a day in my life, so I never learned how to read or write. I can't even read the Bible. I can't teach a Sunday school class. I don't have a good singing voice. I've just more or less sat for years, just warming the pew.

"But I've often thought, *I wish there was something I could do in the church.*"

He continued, "One day I was walking across the church parking lot, and I was saying again to myself and to the Lord, *Isn't there something I could do to help?* Suddenly the Spirit of God arrested me and showed me something I could do. He said to me, 'Do you really want to do something in the church?'

"I said, 'Yes, Lord! Just show me something I can do.'

"The Lord said to me, 'The church doesn't have a janitor, so Brother Hagin usually has to do all the cleaning himself. Why don't you go over and help him by cleaning the church?'

"I said to the Lord, 'Dear God, why didn't I think of that before!'"

I tell you, this man was as proud as if he'd just been elected as the President of the United States. I mean, his face was just beaming the whole time. I thought to myself, *If he'll go through this door that has opened up to him and be faithful in this service, he'll get just as much reward as I will for being faithful in pastoring!*

You see, folks, there is a principle here. God does not reward us according to our *position*. He rewards us according to our *faithfulness*.

God is not going to reward people for the office or position they fill. God is going to reward people for their faithfulness in fulfilling that position. So just be faithful, praise God! There is a door of service that can be opened and is open for you if you'll just ask the Lord to show it to you.

You see, there was a door of service that was open for this man all the time, but he didn't see it. In other words, that door of service was wide open all the time, but he was passing right by it until the Holy Ghost called his attention to it.

And I dare say there are doors of opportunity and doors of service that are open to all believers right now! May the Lord open our eyes so we will see them. Praise God, let's enter through the door of service that the Lord has for us, for not only will others be blessed, but we will be blessed as we obey the Lord!

Doors of Utterance

What other doors does God open for us to serve Him? He not only opens doors of service, but thank God, He also opens doors of utterance.

COLOSSIANS 4:2,3
2 Continue in prayer, and watch in the same with thanksgiving;
3 Withal praying also for us, that God would

**OPEN UNTO US A DOOR OF UTTERANCE, to
speak the mystery of Christ.**

Keep in mind that these Scriptures are written to
the Church — to believers. Paul said to *continue* in
prayer. It is mighty easy to let things distract you until
you are praying just enough to maintain only a mediocre
fellowship with the Lord.

But Colossians 4:2 says, *"Continue in prayer, and
watch in the same with thanksgiving."* Notice that
again and again in the Scriptures the subjects of prayer
and thanksgiving are joined together.

Why? Because when you are praying in faith, you
can thank God in advance, not only for hearing, but
also for answering your prayers.

Now notice especially what Colossians 4:3 says:
*"Withal praying also for us, that God would open unto
us A DOOR OF UTTERANCE. . . ."* Thank God, God
opens doors of utterance. God certainly opened many
doors of utterance for Paul, didn't He? And He will open
doors of utterance for you, too, if you will ask Him to.

Sometimes folks say, "I just can't speak out and be a
bold witness for God." But that is where the baptism in
the Holy Spirit comes in. The Holy Spirit comes to fill
you to give you boldness. We can see this in the Word.

ACTS 1:8 [*Amplified*]
8   But you shall receive POWER — ABILITY,
EFFICIENCY and MIGHT — when the Holy Spirit
has come upon you; and YOU SHALL BE MY WIT-
NESSES . . . to the ends — the very bounds — of
the earth.

When you talk in tongues, the Holy Ghost empowers you to speak supernaturally in other tongues. For example, in Acts 2:4, it says, *". . . they were all filled with the Holy Ghost, and began to SPEAK with other tongues, as the Spirit gave them utterance."*

Those folks who received the Holy Spirit didn't keep quiet — they spoke out in tongues. They spoke in supernatural utterances.

So when you are filled with the Holy Spirit and begin to speak in tongues, the Holy Spirit looses your tongue so you can speak forth in supernatural utterances! And not only does He loose your tongue, but He also empowers you and gives you a boldness you never had before to witness for God.

I remember a lady who received the baptism in the Holy Ghost in one of my meetings. Afterwards, her husband said to her, "What's happened to you? It just seems like you've been turned into another woman!"

Her husband wasn't a Christian, so before she received the baptism in the Holy Spirit, she almost had to follow the Lord secretly. She wasn't bold to speak out about the Lord in her life, and she didn't seem to have any power in her life.

She was what we call a "Milquetoast" Christian. Do you know what I mean by that expression? That means anyone could push her around; she was so timid that she just never stood up for herself or for the Lord. She never witnessed for the Lord or even talked about Him.

Anything her husband wanted to do, they did. But she told me, "When I got baptized in the Holy Ghost,

God gave me boldness. It's like He loosed my tongue, and I could speak boldly for God. I turned into a different person!

"I got so bold, I just simply said to my husband, 'I'm going to church!' Before I received the Holy Ghost, I never would have had the boldness to tell my husband I was going to church."

She told me, "My husband said, 'Well, go ahead if that's what you want to do.'"

She told her husband, "Yes, that's what I want to do. Not only that, but I want to start supporting the church financially."

Her husband was a wealthy fellow. He had plenty of money, and he loved his wife, so he said, "Well, if that's what you want to do, just go ahead and give to the church."

Then he said to her, "Something has happened to you! You used to be so mealymouthed and timid. You never would tell me what you wanted to do. Now you're bold! What's happened to you?"

She said, "I've received the baptism in the Holy Spirit. And the power of the Holy Spirit has changed my life!"

What a difference receiving the Holy Spirit makes in our lives! He opens a door of utterance for us and gives us boldness. He looses our tongue and gives us a *holy* boldness to speak up for God!

Friend, when you think about it, Jesus has opened to us marvelous doors of blessings, provisions, and doors of opportunities for rich spiritual growth, service, and utterance.

May God open your eyes to see God's bountiful doors of blessing and opportunity! Others may not recognize their doors of opportunity, but may you not neglect what God has already prepared for you.

Enter boldly through God's open doors by faith so you can be wonderfully blessed. Entering God's doors of service will greatly enrich your own life, but your obedience will also cause you to be a blessing to humanity! May the eyes of your understanding be opened so you can know God's wonderful abundance in your life!

---

[1] For further study on ministry gifts, *see* Rev. Kenneth E. Hagin's books, *The Ministry Gifts* and *He Gave Gifts Unto Men*.

Chapter 5
The Open Door of Healing

Jesus has already opened doors of blessing for His people. He not only opened the door of salvation, but He also opened the door of *healing* for us. Jesus opened this door, and no man can shut it.

You see, Isaiah prophesied many years ago concerning the coming Messiah that He would bear the sicknesses and diseases of us all. When Isaiah prophesied that in Isaiah 53:4 and 5, he was looking forward into the future.

> **ISAIAH 53:4,5**
> **4   Surely he hath borne our griefs** [sicknesses], **and carried our sorrows** [diseases]: **yet we did esteem him stricken, smitten of God, and afflicted.**
> **5   But he was wounded for our transgressions, he was bruised for our iniquities: the chastisement of our peace was upon him; and WITH HIS STRIPES WE ARE HEALED.**

Isaiah was prophesying about the New Covenant that was to be ratified when Jesus would come to earth and offer Himself as a sacrifice for our sins and bear our sicknesses and diseases.

Then when Peter made his statements concerning the covenant of healing, he was looking back to the stripes that were laid on Jesus' back and back in time to Jesus' sacrifice on Calvary.

1 PETER 2:24
**24 Who his own self bare our sins in his own body
on the tree, that we, being dead to sins, should live
unto righteousness: BY WHOSE STRIPES YE
WERE HEALED.**

Notice this verse doesn't say you are *going* to be
healed — future tense. It says you *were* healed — past
tense. That means in the mind of God, you were already
healed way back at the Cross of Calvary when our sins
and sicknesses were laid on Jesus.

Therefore, the door of healing and health is open
wide to you. Jesus opened it, but it's up to you to enter
through that door! Someone asked, "How do you enter
through the door of healing?" You enter into it by faith
in what God already said in His Word!

How did Jesus open the door of healing for mankind?
By sacrificing Himself! Matthew 8:17 says, ". . . *HIM-
SELF took our infirmities, and bare our sicknesses*"!

First Peter 2:24 said, *"Who his own self bare our sins*
[and sicknesses] *IN HIS OWN BODY on the tree. . . ."*
Jesus not only bore our sins in His own body on the
Cross, but He also bore our sicknesses. Jesus has
already opened the door to healing for us!

That open door of healing is there waiting for you to
go through it. In other words, healing belongs to you *now*.

Just think about it! How do you enter through the
door of salvation? By accepting Jesus as your *Savior*.
Well, how do you enter the door of healing? By accepting Jesus as your *Healer*. You accept Jesus as both your
Savior and your Healer *by faith* in what God already
said in His Word.

Thank God, healing for the physical body is part and parcel of the gospel of our Lord Jesus Christ!

I started preaching divine healing as a young Baptist boy pastor because I saw it in the Word. I had been healed myself, raised up from a deathbed. I had been born into this world sick, and for almost seventeen long years, I never ran and jumped and played like other children.

I was a semi-invalid and became totally bedfast at fifteen years of age and spent sixteen months on the bed of sickness. Five doctors on the case just shook their heads and said, "You've got to die because medical science can't do anything for you."

So for many months, I just lay there, waiting to die. As I lay there dying, I stared at the ceiling in the semi-darkness of death, looking for the open door to healing. But medical science said there was no door open to me. Doctors told me, "We can't do anything for you." According to them, the door to healing was closed to me.

Then I looked to the unbelieving preachers and to the denominational church, and they said that when the last apostle died, he shut the door of healing behind him. They told me, "Healing is not for us today." But, thank God, the last apostle didn't shut the door because no man can shut what Jesus has opened!

Can you imagine (as some church people say, but not Bible-based believers) that when the last apostle died, he shut the door on healing!

Can you picture the last apostle as an elderly gentleman getting ready to die and cross over to the other side to Heaven.

Folks begin to scurry around, saying, "We'd better get to the sick in a hurry, because once this apostle dies, no one else can get healed. We've got to get these sick folks healed in a hurry because that apostle is about to shut the door of healing forever!"

You see, according to what some folks say, that last apostle had the power to shut the door of healing on everyone else who would ever live on this earth. That's foolish, isn't it? And yet that is what many people believe. No, thank God, man can't shut the door of healing. Not even an apostle can shut it. Only Jesus can — but He left it wide open!

What Does God Say About Your Healing?

Just as a teenager on the bed of sickness, something on the inside told me that I could be healed. Mentally, I didn't understand that I could be healed because my mind was filled with religious thinking. My thinking was all cluttered up with the traditions of men.

In other words, I knew what man said about my condition, but not what *God* said! Man said healing had passed away with the last apostle and that I had to die. But thanks be to God, I got into the Word for myself to see what *God* said about healing.

I began reading Grandma's old Methodist Bible for myself. I discovered that the door to healing was wide open! Hallelujah to Jesus! I also found out that what Jesus opens, no man can shut. God never has shut that door of healing and health. It is still open to everyone who will receive healing today.

Men's traditions — "churchianity" — tried to shut the door of healing on me. I discussed the Word with other people. Even some well-meaning church folks and preachers tried to shut the door of healing on me. They said, "No, you can't be healed. The door of healing has been closed. It's shut tight."

But once you find out for yourself the truth of God's Word on healing, no one can shut the door of healing on you! Hallelujah! I'm so glad I found that door wide open!

When I finally got the revelation of divine healing, like a fullback running with the football, I grabbed the Word of God under my arm and took off running with the Word on healing. I made a run for that open door.

Oh, yes, people tried to tackle me and stop me. Everyone told me that door wasn't even there, but I could see it with the eye of faith!

With the truth of God's Word, I had to run as determined as a fullback running down the football field to score a touchdown, dodging unbelievers and knocking down doubt and unbelief!

But thanks be to God! I ran through that open door of healing many years ago. That very door they told me was closed, I found to be open, for Jesus had already opened it by the sacrifice of Himself. I found healing and health.

Now more than sixty years have come and gone, and I'm still healed! And ever since then, I've been going at a hop, skip, and a jump, telling people that the door of healing is still open to them!

Jesus Is the Answer

You see, there may be times medical science won't be able to help people. Some folks will have to look to the Lord to be healed.

Now don't misunderstand me. Thank God for medical science. Thank God for doctors.

In fact, one of the first things I did after I was healed was to make my way to Dr. R_____, one of the five doctors who had been on my case.

I shook hands with him and said, "Dr. R_____, I want to thank you for everything you have done for me. You have just been so wonderful, and I want to thank you for it." He never would charge a penny for his services, but he always went out of his way to help me.

For instance, when I was on the bed of sickness he would say to me: "Son, any time you want me to come to see you, just have your folks call me, night or day. If it is four o'clock in the morning and you need me to come over, just have them call me, and I'll be right over.

"I can't do anything to get you well," he said. "No doctor can do anything to help you. Medically speaking, you will have to die. But if you can get any comfort from my sitting by your bedside, I'll hold your hand and comfort you."

And he was good to his word too. Whenever we would call him, he'd come and try to comfort me. That's why I wanted to go thank him.

Of course, when he found out I'd been healed, he said, "It's just a miracle of God!"

I said, "Yes, it is a miracle of God. But I wanted to tell you that I appreciate you. You sat by my bedside and told me the truth. You said there was nothing you could do to help me medically speaking. You told me, 'Son, just go down the middle of the road and stay ready to go.' But you always took the time to try to help and comfort me."

Well, thank God, I was ready to go as far as being saved was concerned. But when I got into the Word, I found out I didn't have to die. I found out that the door of healing that people said was closed — was really wide open!

But, thank God, the Bible said, "What Jesus opened, no man can shut." The apostles *couldn't* shut the door either because no *man* can shut what Jesus opens. And no denomination has the right or the authority to close the door. The door of healing and health is still open to this day to anyone who wants to walk through that door.

Not only is the door to divine *healing* open, but Jesus has opened the door of divine *health*. What do I mean by that? God not only wants us to be healed if we need healing, but He also wants us to stay in health. I believe Jesus can keep us saved and He can keep us healed too!

One way to stay healed is to walk closely with God every day and stay in close fellowship with Him in His Word. But if you need healing, come to God and receive your healing because Jesus is still the Savior, and He is still the Healer.

God Provided Forgiveness *and* Healing

The psalmist of old said that God provided both forgiveness *and* healing for us. Therefore, the doors of
both forgiveness and healing are already open to us.

PSALM 103:2,3
2   Bless the LORD, O my soul, and forget not all
his benefits:
3   Who FORGIVETH ALL THINE INIQUITIES;
who HEALETH ALL THY DISEASES.

God not only forgives all our iniquities or sins, but
He also heals all our diseases. So if we need healing, we
can appropriate what Jesus has already provided for us.
And what is even better is just to walk in sweet fellowship with Jesus so we can walk in healing and health.

When I first started preaching divine healing, I
didn't know anyone in all the world who believed in
healing except me. I thought I had found something in
the Bible that no one else believed.

I started pastoring my first church when I was eighteen years of age. I accepted the pastorate and preached
my first sermon as a pastor just before I turned nineteen.

I didn't know anyone else who was preaching healing except me. I found out later that a number of folks
preached on healing, but no one encouraged me to
preach on it. In fact, everyone discouraged me and tried
to talk me out of it.

In fact, the denomination I belonged to said, "We
will ordain you if you will just back off a little bit on

this healing business. Now go ahead and preach about prayer if you want to. Go ahead and preach that the Lord hears and answers prayer according to His will. But just back off a little on this healing business, and we will ordain you."

I said, "No, I'm not going to back off on preaching healing. In fact, instead of backing off on it, I intend to preach more on it."

I was preaching healing publicly and praying for people privately, but I intended to start having public healing meetings. You didn't see public healing meetings much in those days. But then I saw that in the Acts of the Apostles and in the four Gospels, Jesus and His disciples held public healing meetings.

Then in 1937, I was baptized with the Holy Ghost and spoke with other tongues. Getting filled with the Spirit wasn't nearly as popular back then as it is now.

In those days, if you spoke with other tongues, you were just automatically kicked out of the mainline denominational churches. So I received the left foot of fellowship from my denominational church, and I came over and aligned myself with Pentecostal folks.

I learned that Pentecostal people preached about divine healing. So I didn't let up on preaching what the Word has to say about healing; I began to preach the truths of God's Word on healing even more.

So at conventions, sectional meetings, fellowship meetings, and youth meetings, I suppose that I preached more than any other preacher in our area. You see, I couldn't sing, so if ministers were going to ask me to do anything, they had to ask me to preach. I would always preach on faith and healing.

Sometimes people would ask me, "Why do you always preach on faith and healing? Don't you know anything else?"

I'd answer, "Certainly I do. You can ask folks in my church. I don't preach on faith and healing all the time in my church. But I do preach on it because it's in the Bible.

"But the reason I preach on faith and healing so much at fellowship meetings and youth rallies is that I want the young people to see the truths of healing like I did as a teenager so they can walk in the light of it. And if I don't preach on it, they would never hear it because you are not preaching it."

Most of them said, "You are exactly right."

Pastors in Full Gospel churches even said to me, "You know, healing is not very important. Healing was just sort of a side issue with the Lord Jesus and with the Apostles."

But if you will search the Scriptures, you will find that Jesus and His disciples not only preached and taught on healing, but they often held healing meetings.

Besides, if you are dying, healing is not a side issue! If you are sick and need healing, healing is not a side issue!

In one meeting I held, the pastor kept saying that to me every day. He'd say, "Well, healing is just a side issue in the New Testament." Finally, in one of my services, I showed that healing was a main issue in the Bible.

I said, "If healing is just a side issue in the New Testament, then Jesus spent three-fourths of His time on a side issue because everywhere He went He taught the people and healed them" (Matt. 14:14; Luke 6:17-19).

Then I said, "And if healing was just a side issue with the Apostles, then in the Acts of the Apostles, they spent most of their time on a side issue."

> **ACTS 5:12,16**
> **12 And by the hands of the apostles were many SIGNS and WONDERS wrought among the people....**
> **16 There came also a multitude out of the cities round about unto Jerusalem, BRINGING SICK FOLKS, and them which were VEXED WITH UNCLEAN SPIRITS: and THEY WERE HEALED EVERY ONE.**

If healing is just a side issue, that means Philip spent much of his time in Samaria on a side issue.

> **ACTS 8:5-7**
> **5 Then Philip went down to the city of Samaria, and preached Christ unto them.**
> **6 And the people with one accord gave heed unto those things which Philip spake, hearing and seeing THE MIRACLES which he did.**
> **7 For unclean spirits, crying with loud voice, came out of many that were possessed with them: and many taken with palsies, and that were lame, WERE HEALED.**

The pastor got up right in the middle of my sermon, and said, "Folks, listen. Brother Hagin has plowed me under.

"He's just plowed me under with the Word." That's a good old Texas expression that means I refuted every one of his arguments.

Then this pastor said, "I've been wrong. I said healing was a side issue of the gospel. But now I see that it is not a side issue; it is the main line." You see, this gospel train runs on two tracks — the new birth and divine healing!

P.C. Nelson was an Assembly of God minister who established Southwestern Bible Institute. He could read and write thirty-two languages and was one of the foremost experts on Greek and Hebrew in the world.

"Dad" Nelson, as we young ministers called him, once said, "Divine healing is part and parcel of the gospel of the Lord Jesus Christ. And what God has joined together, let not man put asunder."

So praise God! Jesus has opened the door of healing for us! I personally would not be alive today except that I learned how to walk through that door of healing for myself.

In the Word we can readily see that God has also provided other methods to help us go through the door to receive our healing.

For example, in Mark 16:17 and 18 Jesus said, "*. . . these signs shall follow THEM THAT BELIEVE; In my name . . . they shall LAY HANDS ON THE SICK, and they shall RECOVER.*"

Who are the signs going to follow? *Those who believe.* Well, what are the signs? One of them is that the believing ones shall lay hands on the sick, and the sick shall recover! Therefore, laying on of hands is one way a person can enter through the door of healing.

Enter the Door of Healing for Yourself

Now listen very carefully to what I'm about to say: I can't enter the door of healing for you, just as you can't enter through that door for me.

But I *can* help inspire you in faith and in your believing so you can go through that door yourself. This is especially true concerning healing, but it also applies to whatever other door of provision or promise Jesus opens for you.

For example, I remember a young lady who was injured in an automobile accident at the age of eighteen. She broke her neck and back in two places, and the doctor said she would never walk again. After two years in the hospital and extensive physical therapy, she could finally swing her body along between crutches for about ten or twelve feet at a time.

She was twenty-eight years old when she came to one of my meetings. Someone carried her into the church and helped her to a pew. I saw her at every service, but she never got in any of the healing lines. Finally one day she asked me, "Brother Hagin, who's going to have faith for my healing — me or you?"

I said, "Both of us. I have to have faith to lay hands on you for your healing in the Name of Jesus. And you have to have faith to receive your healing."

"Well," she said, "if I'm supposed to believe anything, just forget it." After that, she never came back to any more of those meetings to hear me preach.

Two years later, I was holding a series of meetings in the same church and that young lady was there day and night, listening. Then on Friday night of the second week, she came forward and got in the healing line, swinging herself along on her crutches.

I remembered her from two years before, so I said, "Well, I see that you've come."

She said, "Yes, I've come for healing, and I'll be healed too. Just lay your hands on me."

What a vast difference from what she'd said before! You see, before she was trying to get *me* to carry her on *my* faith. But when she came back two years later, *she* was ready to enter the door of healing *herself*.

I just reached my hand out and barely brushed her forehead. I didn't even get to say anything — she just raised both hands and began to praise God for her healing. Both of her crutches fell away, and she walked off totally healed! Glory to God!

Those meetings lasted two more weeks, and from then on she walked two blocks from her house to the church back and forth to services twice every day!

But all those years before she was healed, someone had to drive up to her house and lift her into the car. Then they had to drive up to the side door of the church and lift her out and help her get to the pew on her crutches.

But as soon as she walked through the door of healing for herself, she was totally, one-hundred-percent healed! Then she could walk to church on her own and go wherever she wanted to!

That could have happened two years before, but you see, I couldn't carry her on my own faith. She had to be willing to go through the door of healing herself.

Dear friend, the same is true for you and me. Whether it is the door of healing, salvation, utterance, service, or whatever God has provided for us, every one of us will have to enter through those doors for ourselves!

We can help one another, of course. For example, another believer can come into agreement *with* you in prayer for your healing; others can join their faith with yours. And they can help to *inspire* your faith.

But they can't go through the door of healing *for* you. Jesus Himself can't go through the door for you either. He said, ". . . *behold, I have set before THEE an open door* . . ." (Rev. 3:8).

In other words, Jesus was saying, "I've done My part. I've already paid the price, and I've opened the door for you. Now it is up to *you* to go through it." In the same verse, He even added, "No man can shut that door on you!"

You Can Shut the Door Of Healing on Yourself

Of course, we recognize that Jesus is the One who opens and shuts doors. But when you do not enter an open door, you are in effect shutting the door to that blessing.

Therefore, you can shut the door of healing on yourself. One way you can forfeit your rights to what belongs to you in Christ is by wrong living and wrongdoing.

We find an example of this in the Bible. In fact, Paul talks about a man in the Church in Corinth who was turned over to Satan for the destruction of his body because he wouldn't repent and turn away from his sin.

Evidently this man had taken his stepmother away from his daddy and was living with her in open sin. It is sin to live with a person of the opposite sex without being married. And, apparently, this man was cohabiting with his stepmother!

Today it seems we live in a promiscuous society where immorality is accepted. But living with someone of the opposite sex when you are not married is sin, and believers who do that will eventually be judged by God.

Failure to judge sin and wrongdoing can eventually result in believers being turned over to the devil if they are not careful. They will forfeit their right to the blessings of God that belong to them.

Paul said he was surprised that the Church at Corinth hadn't done anything about this situation.

1 CORINTHIANS 5:1-5
1 It is reported commonly that there is fornication among you, and such fornication as is not so much as named among the Gentiles, that one should have his father's wife.

2 And ye are puffed up, and have not rather mourned, that he that hath done this deed might be taken away from among you.
3 For I verily, as absent in body, but present in spirit, have judged already, as though I were present, concerning him that hath so done this deed,
4 In the name of our Lord Jesus Christ, when ye are gathered together, and my spirit, with the power of our Lord Jesus Christ,
5 To deliver such an one unto Satan for the destruction of the flesh, that the spirit may be saved in the day of the Lord Jesus.

This man didn't judge himself for the sin he was committing, so the Lord had to judge him. He was turned over to Satan for the destruction of his flesh so that his spirit would be saved in the day of the Lord. Later, he did repent and get right with the Lord (2 Cor. 2:6-8). It is not God's best that a person's flesh is destroyed, but it sure beats going to hell.

Then in First Corinthians chapter 11, Paul dealt with the issue of sickness in the Church. He talked about the Lord's Supper and said that believers should judge themselves. When they judge themselves on sin, they won't have to be judged by the Lord.

1 CORINTHIANS 11:26-30
26 For as often as ye eat this bread, and drink this cup, ye do shew the Lord's death till he come.
27 Wherefore whosoever shall eat this bread, and drink this cup of the Lord, unworthily, shall be guilty of the body and blood of the Lord.
28 But LET A MAN EXAMINE HIMSELF, and so let him eat of that bread, and drink of that cup.
29 For he that eateth and drinketh unworthily,

**eateth and drinketh damnation to himself, NOT
DISCERNING THE LORD'S BODY.
30 For this cause many are weak and sickly
among you, and many sleep.**

Paul said, "For this cause many are weak and sickly
among you and many die prematurely." This is talking
about church people — *believers* — dying prematurely!
Their spirits went to be with the Lord, but their bodies
are in the grave.

However, believers don't need to die prematurely.
That isn't God's best. For *what* cause are many believers weak and sickly and die prematurely? Because they
don't examine themselves; they don't judge themselves
on sin. They didn't judge themselves to see whether
they were walking in love toward the Body of Christ.
They didn't examine themselves to see whether they
were partaking of the body and blood of the Lord in an
unworthy manner.

Believers shouldn't be weak and sickly. However,
another reason believers are weak, sickly, and die prematurely is that they don't rightly discern the Lord's body.

Discerning the Lord's body has a twofold applica-
tion. First, believers must discern the fact that the
bread they partake of at the Lord's Supper is a symbol
of the body of Jesus which was broken for their physical
sustenance and healing. By the stripes laid on Jesus'
body, they are healed (1 Peter 2:24).

Second, believers must discern that the body of the
Lord Jesus Christ is a spiritual body. Its members —
the Body of Christ — are one in the Lord. Therefore, if

believers don't walk in love toward their fellow man, eventually the Lord will have to judge them for it.

After all, the Bible says when we don't judge ourselves, the Lord will judge us. Actually, we open ourselves up to the Lord's judgment by our own sin and disobedience.

By not walking in love and by not judging themselves, many believers can get weak, sickly, and can even die prematurely. They are chastened by the Lord, so they won't be condemned with the world.

God Judges Sin

I remember the days of the great Healing Revival. From 1947 through 1958 here in America, there was just a wave of healing. It seemed it was the easiest thing in the world to get people healed.

In fact, some evangelists even said to me, "You know, Brother Hagin, before this Healing Revival began, I never did pray for the sick. I just didn't feel it was my calling. But during the Healing Revival, I began laying hands on the sick, and I just experienced phenomenal success."

They didn't realize it, but laying hands on the sick *was* their calling in the sense that the Bible gives that charge to *all* believers. The Great Commission says, ". . . *lay hands on the sick, and they shall recover*" (Mark 16:18).

However, there was a powerful anointing of healing in those days. And when people tapped into that anointing by faith, many were healed. This same principle holds true in the natural.

For example, in the natural when the wind blows a certain direction, if you throw a piece of paper up in the air, the wind will pick it up and carry it along.

It is the same way in the spiritual realm. If you will just go with the Spirit of God when He is moving a certain direction, you will experience success too. We need to move with the Holy Ghost when He opens a door! However, even during this great Healing Revival when marvelous healings were taking place, some people forfeited their right to the open door of healing because of sin and wrongdoing.

For example, I saw some of the most amazing healings in one evangelist's meeting that I've ever seen. I saw five deaf and mute people get totally healed. I saw crippled people just get up out of wheelchairs and walk off instantly healed.

Yet in spite of all those marvelous healings, God said to me, "You go tell that evangelist that he is not going to live much longer unless he judges himself. The first thing he needs to judge himself on is walking in love toward his fellow man."

This man was thirty-five years old. He didn't judge himself, and by the time he was thirty-eight, he was dead.

Then some people say, "Well, that just means healing isn't for everyone."

But that simply is not true! Jesus opened the door of healing for everyone by the sacrifice of Himself. The door is *wide* open. But people can forfeit their rights to God's promises and provisions by not living right and by not walking in love.

Well, it is just a whole lot better to walk in love and judge yourself. Then you won't be judged by the Lord, and you will be able to walk through that open door of healing.

When you fail to enter through Jesus' open doors because of sin such as doubt, unbelief, or failing to walk in love — you are in effect shutting the doors on yourself. You are closing yourself off from God's wonderful doors of blessings, provisions, and promises.

Jesus is the Opener, and He works on your behalf to open doors for you! Don't close yourself off from the doors He opens! Don't be guilty of hindering the work of the Lord Jesus Christ in your life through sin and disobedience.

Trust the Holy Spirit to help you *see* and *recognize* God's open doors. You can walk through the doors that God has already opened for you! Remember, what God opens, no man can shut.

Actually, you are the only one who can in effect shut the door of God's blessing on yourself. What a pity to shut a door through your own disobedience that God has so freely opened to you!

So by faith and obedience, walk through each door and receive what God has so bountifully provided for you — including healing. Let your life be a testimony to the riches of God's inheritance in Christ. Then you can boldly proclaim God's blessings wherever you go!

Chapter 6
Windows of Heaven

In the previous chapters, I have emphasized two biblical truths. First, Christ is the Authorized One who opens the doors of blessings in our lives. Second, we have a part to play in whether or not we receive those blessings.

In teaching these two biblical truths, I have referred to a number of different symbolic doors or "openings" from the Word of God. But essentially the truths have remained the same: God wants to open doors of blessings in our lives, and we must receive those blessings by faith.

In this chapter, however, I will refer to a different type of opening mentioned in the scriptures in relation to the blessings of God — the windows of Heaven. Although this symbolic opening is a little different from those previously discussed, the truths are basically the same.

Malachi 3:10,11
10 Bring ye all the tithes into the storehouse, that there may be meat in mine house, and prove me now herewith, saith the LORD of hosts, if I will not open you the windows of heaven, and pour you out a blessing, that there shall not be room enough to receive it.
11 And I will rebuke the devourer for your sakes, and he shall not destroy the fruits of your ground; neither shall your vine cast her fruit before the time in the field, saith the LORD of hosts.

In the *New International Version* verse 10 states, ". . . see if I will not throw open the *floodgates* of heaven and pour out so much blessing that you will not have room enough for it."

Notice that the Lord is the One who opens the floodgates of Heaven, but we have a part to play in whether or not we receive those blessings in our lives.

Under what conditions will God open those windows for us? It's as we bring our tithes into the storehouse. That is the condition mentioned in the first part of verse 10: *"Bring ye all the tithes into the storehouse, that there may be meat in mine house. . . ."*

You see, there is a blessing in connection with paying tithes, but first *you* must do your part — *you* must bring them into the storehouse.

However, some people seem to think that God said, "Bring the tithes into the storehouse, and I'll give you just barely enough to get by on. The windows of Heaven will be closed to you, you will almost starve to death, and your children will go hungry."

No! That's not what God said! He said He would bless us abundantly. In fact, He promised to bless us so much that there wouldn't be room enough to receive His blessing!

Malachi 3:10 says *you* have a part to play in getting the windows of Heaven open. How? By paying your tithes and giving offerings. God told us to prove Him regarding the tithe. This is one scripture in which God invites you to prove Him and His Word.

That's how to get blessings poured into your life. But by not rendering your tithes to God, in effect *you* can shut those same windows that God intends to be open to you.

Before I continue to talk about the windows of Heaven and how to receive the blessings of God, I want to say something about the difference between the "open" door of provision that Jesus *has* already "set before us" and the doors He *continues* to open.

I referred to the *open* door of provision as a symbol of the door that the Lord *has* already opened for us through His redemptive work. The open door of God's provisions is available for the believer to receive because of the finished work of Christ. These provisions belong to the believer because of what Jesus has accomplished at the Cross. In other words, the open door represents all that God through Christ provided for us in His great substitutionary work. Therefore, the door of provision is an open door.

Two specific open doors of provision that we already talked about include salvation and the open door of healing. But the provisions of our redemption also include financial blessings.

We see this in the Scriptures. For example, according to Galatians 3:13, *"Christ hath redeemed us from the curse of the law, being made a curse for us. . . ."* And if you read Deuteronomy 28, you find that the curse of the law not only included spiritual death and physical death, but it also included poverty. This means we are also redeemed from the curse of poverty.

In addition, Galatians 3:14 and 29 tells us that Christ came to redeem us so that we might receive the blessing and promise of Abraham. That blessing and provision from God not only includes physical and spiritual blessings, but it also includes financial and material blessing.[1]

Therefore, the open door of provision is an open door to financial blessing. It shows us the truth that God through Christ has given us a way of access into the blessings of God.

But just because there is an open door to financial and material blessings does not mean that everyone is going to appropriate what God has provided for them. Therefore, it is important that we look at this biblical symbol — the windows of Heaven — in order to get a better understanding of our part to receiving the blessings of God.

Tithes Defined

Some would ask, "What is the 'tithe'?" I was preaching about tithes in a church one time, and a fellow asked, "Ties! What are you talking about — crossties or neckties?"

No, tithes does not refer to either one of those! The tithe is a tenth of your income, and it is holy to the Lord.

> **LEVITICUS 27:30,32**
> **30 And all the TITHE of the land, whether of the seed of the land, or of the fruit of the tree, is the Lord's: IT IS HOLY UNTO THE LORD. . . .**
> **32 And concerning the TITHE of the herd, or of the flock, even of whatsoever passeth under the rod, THE TENTH shall be HOLY UNTO THE LORD.**

Also, did you notice that in Malachi 3:10, the Bible says to bring the tithes into the *storehouse*. One fellow came up to me after I taught on the tithe, and said, "I would pay my tithes, but I don't know where the storehouse is."

The "storehouse" simply refers to the local church. So when the scripture says, "Bring ye all the tithes into the storehouse," it means to bring your tithes to your local church where you worship God. You are to bring your tithes to the spiritual storehouse where you receive your spiritual food and blessings.

Tithing Instituted Before the Law

There are some people who say that paying tithes applies only to those who lived under the Law. But, actually, more than 700 years before God gave the Law to Moses, Abraham paid tithes. So tithing can't be just something that was done under the Law.

Then there are other people who say, "I don't believe in that tithe-paying business."

Well, did you ever stop to think that the devil doesn't believe in paying tithes to promote the work of God either? Neither did Hitler, Mussolini, or Stalin. That's mighty bad company to be in agreement with!

Unfortunately, many people just make excuses because they don't want to render the tithe to God. But they are missing out on the blessing of the tithe because this is the only scripture where God ever said we could prove Him on it!

Then other people have another argument for not paying their tithes. They say, "Yes, but paying tithes was for people living under the Old Testament; that's not for us living under the New Testament. After all, you can't argue with the New Testament, and it doesn't say anything about paying tithes." I've looked at them, and thought, *They must not know what the New Testament says about tithing!*

The Lord Jesus Christ Himself put His approval on tithing. Why not just get in agreement with Jesus?

Jesus Endorsed Paying Tithes

There are at least two scriptures to support paying tithes under the New Covenant. First of all, we know Jesus put His endorsement on paying tithes. The Bible says so.

> **MATTHEW 23:23**
> 23 Woe unto you, scribes and Pharisees, hypocrites! for YE PAY TITHE of mint and anise and cummin, and have omitted the weightier matters of the law, judgment, mercy, and faith: THESE OUGHT YE TO HAVE DONE, and not to leave the other undone.

Notice Jesus didn't take sides *against* paying tithes. Also, He didn't say tithes had been done away with.

No, He said, "You *ought* to have paid the tithe, but you also ought *not* to have omitted judgment, mercy, and faith."

Now look at Hebrews 7:8.

HEBREWS 7:8
**8 And here men that die RECEIVE TITHES; but
there he [Jesus] RECEIVETH THEM, of whom it is
witnessed that he liveth.**

I believe this verse applies to Jesus Christ and the
New Testament — the New Covenant. You see, when
you pay tithes and give offerings, some people think
that men here on earth are the only ones receiving your
tithes because it says, ". . . *here MEN THAT DIE receive
TITHES. . . .*"

The phrase "men that die" just means human beings.
That means mortal men receive your tithes on earth.

But that's not all of that verse. Read the rest of it
because the writer of the Book of Hebrews makes a very
profound statement.

The next part of the verse says, ". . . *but there HE
receiveth them, of whom it is witnessed that he liveth*"
(Heb. 7:8).

In our text, Revelation 1:18, Jesus identified Himself as the One who lives forever. He said, *"I AM HE
THAT LIVETH, and was dead; and, behold, I am alive
for evermore. . . ."*

Therefore, even though it *looks* like men are the ones
who receive our tithes here on earth, actually, it is the One
who liveth forevermore who ultimately receives them.

At one of my meetings, a fellow said to me, "Well, I
wouldn't mind paying my tithes to Jesus, but I can't get

up there where He is. I wouldn't mind bringing my tithes into the storehouse, but how am I supposed to get up there to Heaven where the storehouse is?"

I told that fellow, "Jesus is the Head of His Church. And His Church is His Body — the Body of Christ. The Body of Christ is here on this earth.

"Therefore, you can't pay tithes to Jesus Christ the Head of the Church without paying tithes through the members of His Body on this earth.

"For example, you couldn't pay my head one single dime without my hand receiving it first. Well, my hand is a *member* of my body.

"Therefore, if you give your tithe to Jesus, first it is going to have to go to His Body on this earth because the Body of Christ is carrying out the will of Jesus Christ the Head of the Church on this earth."

The Bible is very simple if we will just take it for what it says. But, you see, sometimes we just try to get around doing what it says by making excuses for ourselves.

God Says, 'Prove Me on the Tithe'

Notice something else God said in Malachi 3:10. He said, "*. . . PROVE ME now herewith, saith the LORD OF HOSTS. . . .*"

Do you realize that this is the only scripture where God ever said, "Prove Me"? In fact, the only areas in which God ever said to prove Him are tithes, offerings, and giving.

He invites us to prove this scripture out. He says, "Bring the tithes into the storehouse and prove Me with it. See if I won't open you the *windows* of Heaven."

Now remember, there is a God-ward side and a man-ward side to receiving the blessings of God. In other words, it takes our working together with God to get those windows of His blessing open. When we give, God is faithful to open up the windows of Heaven.

The Bible says what God opens no man can shut. The devil can't shut those windows of blessings on you. *You* are the only one who can shut yourself off from the windows of Heaven, and you do that when you refuse to give of your finances and walk in obedience to the Word.

You see, on the man-ward side, there is something we must *do* if we want to enter God's open doors of blessings or get the windows of Heaven open. Many people are trying to receive God's financial and material blessings with the windows of Heaven closed. Why are the windows closed for some people? Because they haven't done their part through their giving to get the windows of Heaven open and keep them open.

And some people are not living right, so God can't honor their giving; the windows remain closed. They can confess the Word and believe God all they want to, but as long as the windows are closed, the blessings *can't* come. That's often where the problem is.

Folks want God to bless them financially. They want to be increased. And *God* wants to bless them financially and materially. That's what this verse says, "I will pour you out a *blessing* that there shall not be room enough to receive it" (Mal. 3:10). But if people aren't living right, God can't honor their giving.

Obedience and Open Windows of Heaven

You see, sometimes people mistakenly get the idea that faith can just do everything! Don't misunderstand me! I'm not putting down faith; I teach faith in the Bible and in God.

But if we *only* teach faith, we can leave the impression that faith is *all* that is necessary in this Christian walk.

Friend, faith is not the only thing that is necessary to receive the abundance of God's blessings. Faith *and* obedience open God's doors of blessings. For example, just standing on faith confessions alone will not open the windows of Heaven! You are going to have to put some action and obedience to your faith.

Faith is involved in getting the windows of Heaven open, of course. But you won't get the windows of Heaven open *just* by confessing that they are open. In other words, Mark 11:23 alone will not open the windows of Heaven.

MARK 11:23
23 ... whosoever shall SAY unto this mountain, Be thou removed, and be thou cast into the sea; and shall not doubt in his heart, but shall believe that those things which he SAITH shall come to pass; he shall have whatsoever he SAITH.

You can't get the windows of Heaven open just by saying, "Windows of Heaven, be open!" You must put some corresponding action to your faith by being a doer of the Word. You will have to obey what the Word has to say about giving.

Well, what does the Word say? It says to bring the tithes into the storehouse. In other words, you have a part in getting those windows open — there is something you must *do*. In this case, your corresponding action is to render your tithes and then give offerings.

Faith is right and faith in the Word works. But, you see, some folks just emphasize certain parts of faith to the point that some believers think that that's *all* that is necessary to succeed in God. They don't live right, yet they expect their faith to work for them. But that's not in line with the whole counsel of God. God honors *all* of His Word — not just a few select scriptures on faith.

Obedience and the Windows of Heaven

Therefore, even though Jesus has opened all these doors of blessing, provision, and opportunity for us, it takes faith and obedience to walk through those doors. It takes obedience to the Word.

The Bible says, *"Beloved, if our heart condemn us not, THEN have we confidence toward God"* (1 John 3:21). We could read this verse like this: "If your heart condemns you, your faith won't work."

Your faith won't work when you are out of tune with Heaven or out of tune with your fellow man. It will be feeble. But if you walk in the light as He is in the light and you walk in fellowship with others, then your faith will be effective.

> **1 JOHN 1:7**
> **7   But IF WE WALK IN THE LIGHT, as he is in the light, we have fellowship one with another, and the blood of Jesus Christ his Son cleanseth us from all sin.**

Notice that this verse does not say, "If we walk in the light as He is in the light, we have fellowship with those we want to." No, if you are not having fellowship with folks because of strife, unforgiveness, and lack of love, then you are not walking in the light.

I decided a long time ago that I am going to love everyone whether or not they love me. They may not be in fellowship with me, but I am in fellowship with them. You see, failure to walk in love shuts the windows of God's blessings.

I want to emphasize this thought. God tells you that if you want the windows of Heaven open, He will open them if *you* meet certain conditions. What are the conditions to be met? You must walk in obedience to His Word by bringing the tithe into the storehouse. That's *your* responsibility. Then you must continue to walk in line with His Word to keep those windows open.

In other words, you can say that through your obedience to the Word, *you* get the windows of Heaven opened in your life and you keep them open.

Therefore, you have a part to play in getting the windows of Heaven open, and God has *His* part. But God is always faithful to fulfill His part!

So the question is — are you going to be faithful to do *your* part? Through your disobedience, you *can* in effect shut the windows of Heaven on yourself.

Remember that Malachi 3:10 invites you to prove God concerning the tithe.

Malachi 3:10
10 Bring ye all the tithes into the storehouse, that there may be meat in mine house, and prove me now herewith, saith the LORD of hosts, if I will not open you the windows of heaven, and pour you out a blessing, that there shall not be room enough to receive it.

You may not know a lot about faith, but you can still obey God by walking in the light you do have and bringing His Word before Him. So continue to take God at His Word, get those windows of Heaven open, and *keep* them open!

Rebuking the Devourer

In this passage on tithing, Malachi 3:11 shows that God is talking about financial and material blessing. It says, *"And I will rebuke the devourer for your sakes, and he shall not destroy the fruits of your ground . . ."* (Mal. 3:11).

People made their living in Malachi's time by the fruit of their ground and by the yield of their vineyards. The verse also goes on to say, *". . . neither shall your vine cast her fruit before the time in the field, saith the Lord of hosts."* You see, part of the blessing of the tithe is that God promised to rebuke the devourer for our sakes.

I knew a man personally, Brother S_____, whom I worked for part time when I first started preaching out in the country.

You wouldn't think it just to look at him and talk to him because he worked every day just as hard as anyone did, but he was a very wealthy man.

He was worth probably one or two million dollars. This man not only had a lot of money, he also owned houses and lands.

The windows of Heaven were open in this man's life. What was the secret of his success? I personally asked him that question. I'd heard his story from others, but I wanted to hear it from him firsthand, so I asked him the secret of his success.

Brother S_____ said to me, "Brother Kenneth, I'll tell you exactly how I got started. I didn't have anything much. I was just a farmer. I had a farm, but it wasn't even paid for. Then I leased some additional land that I was working too.

"I supported the church; I gave liberally. Actually, we didn't have a lot of needs in the church. We had a new brick church building, and the church was well off financially. But one day a missionary came to our church who needed financial support for a special project.

"I knew something about the missionary through some friends, and I decided to give toward this need. I didn't really have any kind of leading at all about giving to this missionary project. I just gave by faith because I believed God, and I knew this missionary had a great need."

Now this was in Texas, and in those days cotton was king. In other words, cotton was the major crop. But farmers didn't have all the sprays and insecticides they've got now, so the boll weevil destroyed many a crop. The boll weevil is an insect that attacks the cotton boll. In those days, sometimes complete cotton fields were destroyed by this insect.

But do you know what happened to the farm and the land that Brother S_____ was working? The boll weevils destroyed everybody else's crop, but they just piled up against his fence! They never got on his land. That's a historical fact!

You see, in regard to tithing, the Bible says in Malachi 3:11, "I will rebuke the devourer for your sake." God rebuked the devourer for Brother S_____! Why? Because he not only tithed and believed God for the blessing of the tithe, but he also gave liberal offerings.

I heard about this incident as a little boy. People all over were talking about how all those boll weevils just stacked up all along Brother S_____'s fence! I heard about this before I ever met Brother S_____.

On Sundays, people from all around that part of the country would drive out there to see that. It looked like a parade of people passing by Brother S_____'s farm and his land. People almost couldn't believe what they saw!

Brother S_____ didn't have any chemicals or sprays or anything to fight against the boll weevil, yet his fields still produced a bountiful crop that year. In fact, he made more than $100,000 that year alone!

Why do you suppose that happened? Because God honored his giving. Brother S_____ not only tithed, but he also gave liberally in offerings. God always honors faith in His Word.

I don't know about you, but I just like the way Malachi 3:10 reads: "Bring the tithes into the storehouse, and I'll open the windows of Heaven and *pour* you out a blessing." Glory to God!

According to the margin notes of my Bible, in the Hebrew, the word "pour" is translated *to empty out* a blessing. In other words, God will *empty out* or *pour out* a blessing on you that there shall not be room enough for you to receive!

Imagine getting blessed so much that you'd have to say, "Lord, I can't take any more blessing! Just turn it off. There's no room to receive any more blessing!" In this verse, God is talking about pouring out upon you material and financial blessings.

Some folks say, "Well, I'm going to get blessed like that!" and they give just from a natural, selfish standpoint. The only reason they give is in order to get blessed. Well, that kind of giving is not going to work if the attitude of their heart isn't right.

No matter how much people give or how faithfully they pay their tithes, if people give just to consume the blessing upon themselves, it's not going to work. Why? Because they are over in the area of selfishness.

You see, we've all heard a lot of preaching against sin. For example, people preach against lying, stealing, cheating, robbing, and so forth. And it is true, all those things are wrong. But, my friend, wrong motives are just as wrong, and God will judge His people on the motives of their hearts too!

----

[1]For further study on redemption, *see* Rev. Kenneth E. Hagin's book, *Redeemed From Poverty, Sickness, and Spiritual Death.*

Chapter 7
Motives and Giving

Years ago, an evangelist I knew kept saying to me, "You ought to write a book! You could really make money!"

Because he said this, it was years before I actually did write a book. I knew that if I ever wrote a book to make money, I would be in trouble with the Lord. I did not want to write a book until I was absolutely certain that I was only doing it to help people. That had to be my only motive.

God promised to bless us, and we need to know that. We need to remember and believe that, but sometimes there is a fine line that has to do with the motives of our heart. Actually, as far as we are concerned, we can close the windows of Heaven on ourselves if our motives continue to be impure.

First of all, people ought to give because they love the Lord! They should give because they love souls and want to promote the Kingdom of God and the work of God.

They should be able to say, "I'm going to give to help and benefit others even if I never receive anything in return." When people can make that statement of commitment, they know their motives are pure. And when people do give from pure motives and they believe God and love the Lord, God will honor their giving.

Pure Motives Bring Promotion in God

I've seen people just be blessed financially through their giving even though they didn't know much about faith or believing God. But they lived right, and their motives for giving were pure. They wanted to bless people and promote the Kingdom of God.

For example, I remember one fellow in particular who was a minister back in the Depression days in the '30s. He knew very little about faith as such, yet he became wealthy. Although he didn't know it, he was actually acting on faith principles.

This was in Depression days. You've got to realize that during the Depression, men would work all day long — not just eight hours, but from sunup until sundown — to earn $1.

And when I started preaching, there were men with families in my church who made $37.50 a month. That was their total salary for the whole month!

They would pay their house rent, utilities, any other expenses, and feed their families on that salary!

Of course, things were less expensive back then. For example, you could buy a Cadillac for $700 or $800. You could buy a Ford for about $400. You could buy a loaf of bread for a nickel, and a gallon of gasoline cost a nickel.

In those days to impress their girlfriends, fellows would drive up to the gasoline pump, and say, "Fill 'er up!" At the same time, they'd hold their hand out the window where the girl couldn't see it, and just hold up one finger to show the gasoline attendant they really wanted just one gallon of gasoline!

That would really impress a fellow's girlfriend because folks didn't have much money in those days. A fellow would be doing well to be able to buy a whole tank of gasoline at one time!

Anyway, this minister I knew said something profound to me. He said, "Brother Hagin, I really don't know much about exercising faith. For instance, I really don't know how to exercise my faith to get healed. But even in the trying times of the Depression, I always owned a brand-new automobile. In fact, I was never without a new car."

He said, "Financially speaking, my family never suffered even though we pastored some small churches. We only ran 60 or 70 people on Sunday morning, but we never went without financially. We always lived in a nice house and had plenty to eat; we never suffered financially."

Why did he always have plenty even in Depression days? Why was he always well provided for even when others experienced lack and went without? Because he always kept the windows of Heaven open in his life. How? He not only paid his tithes, but he was a great giver.

Think about it! This minister always drove a new car. He wore new clothes. He lived in the best of homes, and his family always dressed in the best — even in Depression days! He never had financial problems even though many times he pastored small churches.

But he tithed and gave generously to advance the work of God. That was the secret of his success. He put himself in position to receive the blessings of God.

The Man Who Became A Millionaire in Depression Days

I knew another fellow down in Texas who never did get beyond the fifth grade in education. He dropped out of school to go to work. He never wore a pair of shoes until he was twelve years old. His folks were so poor, they lived in a little one-room cabin down in east Texas.

As a child, this fellow never owned any store-bought clothes. His Momma would take clothes other people gave her and remake them for him. And in the fall of the year, she would take a cotton feed-sack and make him a pair of britches to wear to school.

But do you know that when this man grew up, he made it big and was worth more than a million dollars in Depression days! That was practically unheard of. I mean, back in Depression days when times were hard, if you had a million dollars, you were really rich. There weren't many rich folks around.

Do you know how he got there? I knew the fellow personally, and I talked to him about it. He didn't know very much about faith, but he did know a little bit about it.

However, he knew how to get God to open up the windows of Heaven by obeying the Word on giving. He got the windows of Heaven opened up early in his life,

and those windows were never closed on him. Why?
Because *he* kept them open by his giving.

On God's side, God kept them open because this
man obeyed His Word on giving (Mal. 3:10; Luke 6:38).
And the Bible does promise us a return on our giving.

> **PROVERBS 3:9,10 (*Amplified*)**
> 9   Honor the Lord with your capital and suffi-
> ciency [from righteous labors], and with the
> FIRST FRUITS [tithe] of all your income;
> 10 SO SHALL YOUR STORAGE PLACES BE
> FILLED WITH PLENTY, and YOUR VATS BE
> OVERFLOWING WITH NEW WINE.

God promised to fill our storage places with plenty!
He said our vats would be overflowing with new wine. I
don't know about you, but I want the abundance the
Lord promises!

You see, God has told us exactly how to get the windows of Heaven open! It's through our giving to the
work of God. In Malachi, God even promised that He
would pour us out a blessing in such a measure that
there would hardly be room enough to contain it.

God doesn't make empty promises. What He has
said in His Word, He is able to perform (Rom. 4:21). The
Bible also says that God is not a man that He should
lie. He is faithful to His Word.

> **NUMBERS 23:19**
> 19 God is not a man, that he should lie; neither
> the son of man, that he should repent: HATH HE
> SAID, AND SHALL HE NOT DO IT? or HATH HE
> SPOKEN, AND SHALL HE NOT MAKE IT GOOD?

Since God's Word is true and can be depended upon, then let's be doers of the Word so we can get those windows open!

Giving to the Poor

Now this man down in Texas who became a millionaire in Depression days didn't give generously just to get. He didn't have a stingy, graspy attitude, giving just to get everything he could.

No, that fellow was one of the most generous persons I have ever met in my life. Whenever he would see anyone in need, he always helped them. He gave generously because he wanted to see the work of God promoted and advanced. In other words, his motives for giving were pure.

So not only did he render his tithes and give offerings, but he was a great one to give to the poor. He believed and stood on the promise of Proverbs chapter 19.

> **PROVERBS 19:17 (*Amplified*)**
> **17 He who has pity on the POOR lends to the Lord, and that which he has given HE WILL REPAY TO HIM.**

Sometimes I think believers read this verse, "He who lends to the Lord, the Lord will just forget about it." No! That's not what the Bible says. The Lord will do what? The Lord will *repay* him. The Bible also said, *"He that hath a bountiful eye shall be blessed . . ."* (Prov. 22:9).

You see, giving to the poor is over and above giving tithes and offerings. Don't take your *tithes* and give

them to the poor. Your *tithe* belongs in the storehouse —
in your local church home. But then after you have
given to your church, the Bible also talks about giving
alms to the poor.

> **LUKE 12:33**
> **33 Sell that ye have, and GIVE ALMS; provide
> yourselves bags which wax not old, a treasure in
> the heavens that faileth not, where no thief
> approacheth, neither moth corrupteth.**

The Bible says that if you give to the poor, you are
actually lending to the Lord. And the Lord will repay
you. This is one of the ways to keep those windows of
Heaven open in your life.

Beware of Con Artists

The Bible talks about giving to the poor. But giving
to the poor doesn't mean giving to folks who just pre-
tend to have a need in order to con money out of people.
We call them "panhandlers" and "con artists."

Some people just live off everyone else. If you let
them, folks like that will sponge off you. God will reveal
those kinds of people to you. God never said a word
about giving con artists anything.

There are religious con artists who will try to con
Christians out of anything they can. But that is not
what this verse in Proverbs 19:17 is talking about. It is
talking about people with bona-fide needs.

You see, when you are really walking by faith, you
don't go around telling everyone your needs. Other people

aren't the ones who are supposed to open the windows of Heaven for you! God is! And you make it possible by your tithing and giving.

I have never in my life told others about my own personal financial needs or even suggested I needed anything. I just believed God for it. Real faith is believing that God alone is your Source.

Now as far as ministry is concerned, it is all right to let people know about a project or a ministry need and let them give if they want to (1 Cor. 16; 2 Cor. 9). But it's not right to pressure people into giving.

You don't look to people to open doors and windows of God's blessings for you. *Jesus* is your Opener! God very clearly tells you in His Word how to get those windows of Heaven open for yourself. It is God's will that you learn how to get those windows open yourself. You do it by your obedience to what the Word says about giving and you keep them open by living right.

One ditch some people have fallen into is they have the impression that no matter how they live or whether or not they've dealt with sin in their life, if they'll just *give*, God will multiply their giving and give back to them.

No, He won't. God honors all of His Word, not just a part of it. Tithing and giving is one side of getting the windows of Heaven open. But there is another side to it. You still have to live right; you still have to walk in love and live according to the principles in God's Word. You won't get very far in God without living right.

GALATIANS 6:7
7   Be not deceived; God is not mocked: for WHAT-

SOEVER A MAN SOWETH, that shall HE ALSO
REAP.

Now Paul didn't write this verse to sinners. He
wrote it to Christians. Paul was telling Christians not to
be deceived about God's laws of sowing and reaping.
Whatsoever a man sows, *that* shall he also reap.

Now the law of sowing and reaping applies in every
area of life, not just in the financial area. But it is certainly true that if you sow finances, you will reap a
return.

Ill-Gotten Riches Won't Last

There are some folks who thought that God was
going to prosper them, so they sowed their finances just
for that purpose. But they weren't living right. In fact,
they got what money they had by being crooked.

Then they said, "I'm going to put this money in the
offering, and God will honor it because I heard the pastor say God honors giving." But God didn't honor it. God
honors it when people walk in the revealed light of His
Word in every area. A person can't expect God to honor
his giving when he consciously continues to violate
God's Word in other areas.

For example, I know one man, and it doesn't sound
big now, but many years ago when money was still
money, this man was a millionaire. When you had that
much money back then, it could possibly be like being a
billionaire today. He was very wealthy.

I visited him in his home. He lived in a palatial home for the day — I mean way beyond what anybody else owned. And in those days not too many people drove Mercedes, Lincolns, or Cadillacs. But both he and his wife each owned their own personal luxury car.

Their son and daughter each had their own personal luxury car too. He also owned a private jet, and he was very liberal about giving. Yet his prosperity didn't last; he lost everything he had.

Well, why didn't his prosperity last? After all, he did pay his tithes. And he gave liberal offerings. But, you see, many of his business deals just weren't quite right. In other words, they were crooked, or at least just a little unethical or illegal.

Therefore, he wasn't in a position spiritually to receive from God. God couldn't honor his giving.

Well, that affected him spiritually, and it affected him financially and materially. It even affected him physically. He and his wife were both sick.

So, you see, the whole package goes together, doesn't it? Tithing and giving offerings get the windows of Heaven open, but you also have to live right to be in a position so God *can* bless you. Can you see that?

Down in Texas years ago, I also knew another fellow. I noticed he never had anything in life. The soles of his shoes were always worn out. He never seemed to have a dime in his pocket. I began to watch this fellow's life to see why he was always so destitute. He just never seemed to prosper in anything.

I found out that this fellow was really a religious con. He would intentionally get close to people he knew who had money. For example, on Sunday nights, we used to close our services by gathering around the altar to pray.

This particular man would get around those people he knew who had money, and he'd pray out loud: "Lord, You can see the soles of my shoes are worn out. These are the only shoes I have. Oh, Lord! Lay it on someone's heart to buy me a new pair of shoes."

Well, very often the person praying at the altar next to him would look at the man's shoes, and sure enough, they were worn out. The person would feel sorry for him, so he'd buy him a pair of shoes. Then the fellow would go away saying, "The Lord met my need!"

Actually, he lied about it. The Lord wasn't the one who met his needs. He *conned* people into meeting his needs! That's not faith. He didn't exercise any faith at all. That wasn't an example of the windows of Heaven being opened to him. And he wasn't a doer of the Word. He was really just fooling people into buying things for him.

This man would also go visit revival meetings where he knew there were people in that church who had money, and he'd make sure he got around them.

When they went to the altar to pray as the custom was in those days, he would make sure he got right beside them and prayed out loud: "Lord, You can see that my suit is all frayed. It's the only one I've got. Lord, lay it on someone's heart to buy me a new suit."

When some kind person would offer to buy him a suit, he'd go off saying, "My faith is really working!" But his faith wasn't working at all. He was lying.

If he had really been using his faith, he could have claimed a new suit or a new pair of shoes in private so that only God knew about it. And if he had been living right and had based his petition on the Word, he would have received his answer too!

Friend, when you are walking by faith, you don't have to con people into giving to you. You give because you love the work of God. When your giving and your faith line up with the Word of God, then you're in a position to receive God's best! And even when you don't have a dime, you can keep a smile on your face and keep shouting the victory.

I know. I've been there. Many times I just acted like I had plenty of money. I didn't tell anyone I didn't have a dime, because my faith was in God and His Word.

You see, I knew that Jesus is the One who opens the windows of Heaven. He is the One who supplies all my needs, so I don't acknowledge my need to man; I acknowledge Jesus' abundant supply.

Actually, this man was a professional moocher. Once I found out what he was doing, I watched his life. Do you know that in the natural, he never did have anything. And he never prospered spiritually.

You see, you can't prosper when you are dishonest. God won't open the windows of Heaven and pour you out His financial blessings when you are cheating other people!

This man wasn't living a life of giving because he loved to give to the work of God. His motives were all wrong. How could God open the windows of Heaven for him? He couldn't. As we used to say, this man wasn't living "under the spout where the glory comes out"!

In other words, he wasn't living in the blessings of God. He was living in the soulish realm, motivated by the flesh. He was really living in sin because he was always trying to con the Body of Christ into giving to him.

But all his empty prayers didn't move God's hand of blessing on his life, because God can't put His approval on dishonesty. Therefore, the windows of Heaven were never opened to him.

On the other hand, remember this other minister I told you about who pastored small churches yet prospered greatly? He really was walking by faith, whether he knew about all the principles of faith or not.

He was walking by faith because he was walking in obedience to the Word, particularly in the area of giving. And the Word worked for him. Therefore, the windows of Heaven could be opened in his life. And he learned how to keep them open.

We need to get to the place in our faith where we believe God is *who* He says He is and that God will *do* what He says He will do. And then we must obey the Word and walk in the light.

Also, we need to believe that we are *who* God says we are and that we can do *what* God says we can do. One thing we can do is obey God's Word so the blessings of God can be poured out in our lives. When we obey God's Word, God will honor us because He honors His Word (1 Sam. 2:30).

If you've got the windows of Heaven open in your life, it doesn't matter what happens in this world. No matter how bad inflation gets or whether there is a recession, the windows of Heaven will still be open in your life. I saw that in the lives of these two men who prospered that I told you about.

I'm so glad I learned how to get the windows of Heaven open! And do you know what? *The devil can't shut the windows of Heaven!* Oh, he'll try to, but he can't shut them. But your disobedience can shut them.

What's more, no man can shut the *windows* or floodgates of Heaven any more than man can shut any *door* that Jesus opens for you. What God opens, no man can shut — whether it is a door or a window.

You are the only one who can close yourself off from the windows or doors of Heaven. Through disobedience and failing to walk in the light of the Word of God, you can in effect shut the doors and windows on yourself.

So let's get the windows of Heaven open in our lives so we can enjoy the blessings of God and be a blessing to humanity! Let's learn the secret of obeying God in giving, and then watch Him open the windows of Heaven!

Chapter 8
Offerings Open
The Windows of Heaven

Giving offerings is one way we obey God so He can open the windows of Heaven. Notice the full context of that passage in Malachi chapter 3. God was not just speaking of tithes but of offerings too.

> **MALACHI 3:8,9**
> **8 Will a man rob God? Yet ye have robbed me. But ye say, Wherein have we robbed thee? In TITHES and OFFERINGS.**
> **9 Ye are cursed with a curse: for ye have robbed me, even this whole nation.**

Evidently the Israelites had neglected their tithes and offerings because God said to them: "You've robbed Me in tithes and offerings." Then He said, *"Ye are cursed with a curse: for ye have robbed me. . . ."*

Well, we don't want to be under a curse because we've robbed God in our tithes and offerings. We want to walk in the blessings of those open windows of Heaven!

You see, we are supposed to give to God both in tithes *and* in offerings. The tithe *belongs* to God (Mal. 3:10). Once I render my tithes, then I consider my offerings to be *giving* to God.

Thank God, we have something to do with getting the windows of Heaven open in our lives as we live down here on this earth.

Get those windows of Heaven open and keep them open so you can receive the blessings of God!

Give and It Shall Be Given Unto You

Now look for a moment at a New Testament verse about giving that we often quote. It certainly does apply to us. And Jesus Himself said it.

> **LUKE 6:38**
> 38 Give, and it shall be given unto you; GOOD MEASURE, PRESSED DOWN, and SHAKEN TOGETHER, and RUNNING OVER, shall men give into your bosom. For WITH THE SAME MEASURE THAT YE METE withal IT SHALL BE MEASURED TO YOU AGAIN.

This verse says that if you give, it will be given back to you *good* measure. But that verse doesn't stop there. Notice how your blessing will be returned to you: Not just good measure, but *pressed down, shaken together,* and *running over*!

That sounds like the blessings of the tithe in Malachi, doesn't it? Malachi 3:10 says there would not be room enough to receive or contain the blessings of God.

Here in Luke, we're told the blessings will be pressed down, shaken together, and running over. Both of those scriptures are describing an abundance of the Lord's blessings.

That sounds good, doesn't it? But Luke 6:38 doesn't even stop there. Then it continues, saying, ". . . *For with the same measure that ye mete withal it shall be measured to you again*"! Therefore, *you* have something to do with the measure that is given back to you!

I remember that on one occasion I was preaching in Texas. A friend of mine who lived in the particular city where I was holding the meeting contacted me and asked me to come by his house before the service.

I stopped by his house, and in the course of our fellowshipping together, he handed me a one-hundred-dollar bill. In fact, on two different occasions during the time I was preaching in that city, this man gave me an offering of a one-hundred-dollar bill each time.

You have to realize that back then, people didn't give hundred-dollar bills away because most people didn't have hundred-dollar bills! You very seldom even received a five- or ten-dollar bill in an offering. In those days, offerings mostly consisted of one-dollar bills or change.

Anyway, this man didn't say much about it, except to explain, "Brother Hagin, I give my tithes to my own church, so this isn't part of my tithe. I just want to give you an offering over and above my tithe."

Then as we were driving to the church, he asked me, "Have you ever preached on Luke 6:38?"

I said, "No, I haven't, at least not just taking that one verse for a text. I've referred to it in sermons, of course."

"Well," he said, "an evangelist held a two-week revival in our church. He read Luke 6:38 for his text every single night for two solid weeks."

He continued, "Do you know what? We had one of the best revivals we've ever had in that church. People were saved every single night. That evangelist had one of the best salvation responses we've ever had in a revival meeting."

Then my friend said, "The last night of the meeting, the pastor took up an offering for this evangelist. But then the evangelist got up and read Luke 6:38 again, and said, 'Folks, I've read every night from this text. And I'm going to receive an offering tonight for this church because this building needs a new air-conditioning system.'"

This was many years ago now, but the people had bought this building and converted it into a church. Actually, the air-conditioning in that church was a pre-World War II system that finally just broke down.

If you've ever been to Texas, you know how hot it gets in the summertime. So this church really did need a new air-conditioning system. In fact, they needed about $10,000 for a new system. That doesn't sound like much now, but back then it was a lot of money.

The evangelist said, "I'm just going to open my Bible to Luke 6:38 and lay it down here on the altar. And I'm going to encourage you to give an offering based on Luke 6:38. This offering will go exclusively for a new air-conditioning system for this church."

Because the Lord was leading him to take this special offering he said, "I don't want any of you to give anything you *can* afford to give. I want you to give what you think you *cannot* afford to give."

The evangelist continued, "The Word of God says, 'Give and it shall be given to you, good measure, pressed down, and shaken together, and running over.' I know God doesn't lie."

My friend who was relating this to me said, "I was sitting in that service, and I thought, *Now wait a minute! That evangelist said to give what we cannot afford to give.* So I just decided to give everything I had, which wasn't a whole lot."

My friend told me, "Actually, I gave all the money I had that was to last me for the next week. I didn't have a dime left to buy groceries.

"I said to myself, *I hope my wife has some food in the pantry, because I just emptied my billfold and put everything I had in that offering.*"

This fellow told me, "I taught a men's Bible study at the church during the week. Before this evangelist came to town, two men in the Bible study had come to me privately after one of the Bible study sessions. They were businessmen, and they wanted me to pray for them.

"They were broke, and they'd each been advised by their financial advisors to file for bankruptcy on their businesses because they were both in such bad shape financially."

My friend continued, "These two men also gave in the offering that night. I knew they couldn't afford to give, any more than I could afford to give the money I put in the offering.

"But I am a witness to the fact that in thirty days, both of those fellows' businesses were out of the red and in the black! They immediately began to prosper." The windows of Heaven were opened and God's blessings were being poured out on them.

Can God Use Sinners to Bless Us?

This man who was talking to me as we drove to the church service was a carpenter. The windows of Heaven were being opened on him too.

He related one incident that happened to him as a result of his giving. He said, "On the job where I worked, I needed a particular carpentry tool. I'd priced that tool thinking maybe I could buy one, but I couldn't afford it; it was just too expensive.

"One of the fellows who worked with me had bought this particular tool. He wasn't a Christian, but sometimes I'd borrow his tool. But on the Monday after I'd given in that offering, I was out on the job working, and this sinner man came around and laid this expensive tool down beside me." This tool was quite an expensive piece of equipment for that day.

"He said to me, 'I want to give you this tool.'" Imagine that! A sinner man!

But notice what Jesus said, "Give, and it will be given unto you, good measure, pressed down, shaken together, running over — shall *men* give into your bosom."

Who will give to you? *Men* shall give to you — that means people. In other words, the Bible doesn't say that it will only be Christians who will give to you. God can use sinners to bless you too — men and women alike!

This brother said to me, "I asked that sinner man, 'Why do you want to give me your tool?'"

"He said, 'I don't know. I just don't know! I was up on top of the house putting on the roof, and something just came over me. And before I knew it, I said to myself, *I'm going to give that fellow that tool!'*

"Then that unsaved man asked me, 'Will you take it?'

"I said, 'I sure will!'"

God can use sinners to bless us! After all, the Bible does say *men* will give into our bosom.

Let me tell you something that happened to Uncle Bud Robinson who was an old-time Methodist preacher in Texas at the turn of the century. He and his wife and three children lived out in the country. Uncle Bud regularly gave tithes and offerings.

One morning Uncle Bud got up and discovered that they didn't have a bite of food to eat in the house, not even one crumb of bread. He and his family sat down at the table in faith just like they had food to eat. They thanked God and prayed, but they didn't have a crumb of bread or a drop of milk!

Uncle Bud said, "Just by faith I said to my family, 'Well, I'm going to hook up the buckboard and go into town.'" In those days people cooked with a wood stove, so he said to his wife, "Keep the stove hot. I'm going to bring back a bill of groceries, and we'll have a feast."

In his autobiography, Uncle Bud said, "I said that by faith. I didn't know where food would come from, but I just believed God."

So Uncle Bud hooked up the buckboard, went into town, and tied the horses' reins up to the hitching rail. In those days towns had boardwalks that were made out of wood. Uncle Bud started walking down that boardwalk, and back then, they still had open saloons in the towns and cities.

Uncle Bud said, "I was walking down this boardwalk, and all of a sudden a drunk came stumbling out of a saloon, just weaving all over the boardwalk. About the time he got to me, he stopped dead still."

The drunk man said to him, "Hey! Uncle Bud!"

He knew Uncle Bud, because Bud was the local preacher in those parts. The drunk man reached both hands into his coat pocket and pulled out two fistfuls of silver dollars. Now you've got to understand that money went a long way back in those days. They didn't have inflation like we do today; money was worth a lot more then than it is now.

The drunk man said, "Here, Uncle Bud! Here! Take this and go buy yourself something to eat. We're not going to let you starve! Go buy some groceries."

Uncle Bud said, "I reached my hands out and took all that money. Then the drunk went on down the street just singing."

Uncle Bud said, "I went and bought groceries. In fact, in those days, you could buy so many groceries with that amount of money, I filled up the whole buck-board with food! I went back home just singing."

Uncle Bud said, "Somebody asked me, 'Do you think God spoke to that drunk?'

"Why, certainly!" he answered. "He sure did. In the first place, how did that drunk know I didn't have any food? He said to me, 'Here, go buy some groceries. We're not going to let you starve.' How else did he know that?"

Notice that Luke 6:38 says, "Give, and it shall be given unto you; good measure, pressed down, and shaken together, and running over, shall *men* give into your bosom." That means mankind. It doesn't say a thing in the world about Christians being the only ones to give to you!

Jesus didn't say, "Only fellow Christians will give into your bosom," or "Believers you know will give into your bosom." No, Jesus said, "*Men* shall give into your bosom" — that means mankind — saved and unsaved alike.

'You Can't Out-Give God!'

There is a sequel to what happened to the man who gave me the two one-hundred-dollar offerings. He related something else that happened to him as a result of his giving.

He said to me, "I've been wanting a new car, so I decided I'd trade my old car in and get a better one. I went out to a car lot, and I looked at the cars.

"There was one in particular that I wanted, but it was a brand-new car. As I looked it over, I thought to myself, *That's just too big of a step for me financially. My monthly payment would be too much.* So instead I selected a used car. I thought, *Well, at least it's an upgrade of a year or two.*

"Finally, a salesman came over and asked if he could help me. I said, 'Yes, I'm looking at this used car, and I want to trade mine in on it and finance the rest.'

"The salesman said to me, 'I saw you looking at that new car over there a while ago.'

"I told the salesman, 'Yes, but that's just too big of a step for me financially. I can only handle so much a month, and that would just be too expensive for me.'

"The salesman said to me, 'Well, I own this car lot, so I'll tell you what I'm going to do. I'm going to let you have that new car for just what I've got in it. I won't make anything on it, and I'll take your car in for top value, so your payments will be less than what you thought they would be.'"

My friend told me, "I could hardly believe it! But then I remembered what Luke 6:38 said, 'Give, and it shall be given unto you; good measure, pressed down, and shaken together, and running over, shall *men* give into your bosom.'"

My friend told me, "As that salesman was signing the papers on the deal, I finally asked him, 'Why do you want to do this for me?'

"He said, 'I don't know why. Something just told me to. And since I decided to do it, I just feel so good about it that I'm glad I did it!'"

Then my friend said to me, "You know, Brother Hagin, I'm having the biggest time I ever had in my life giving to help the work of God. I've got more money now by giving than I've ever had before in my life.

"I pay my tithes, don't misunderstand me. The money I give to people is offerings; I put my tithes in my local church."

He said, "But every week, I just seek out somewhere that I can give. I'm giving away more in offerings than I ever have in my life, but I'm receiving more money than I've ever had in my life too. The more I give, the more I get, and I'm having the biggest time blessing folks that I've ever had in my life!"

You see, this man wasn't just giving to get. It's all right to give in faith and expect a return. But that wasn't his main motive. He wanted to bless people and see the work of God promoted. God will always honor His Word.

Friend, you can't out-give God! So do you want the doors and the windows of Heaven open for you? God tells you exactly how to get them open. Walk in obedience to His Word in this matter of tithes *and* offerings.

One prayer that has enriched my life is this: "Lord, make me a blessing wherever I go."

When your motive is to bless others, and you are obeying God in tithes and offerings, God will be faithful to His Word. He will open those windows of Heaven so you can be a blessing to mankind. You can't out-give God!

Chapter 9
The Open Doors of Heaven

Our Lord and Savior Jesus Christ opens doors for us no man can close! The Bible says that Jesus has set before us an *open* door. Christ has given us free access to His provisions and promises. Therefore, we need to discover how to enter through every one of the doors Jesus has so richly provided for us.

The Lord opens up people's hearts and opens the eyes of their understanding (Acts 16:14; Eph. 1:18). He's opened the wonderful door of healing and health. He opens the door of the Word and opens doors of opportunity and doors of service for us (Luke 24:32; 1 Cor. 16:9). He opens the windows of Heaven and pours blessings into our lives.

Jesus also opens to us the door of utterance that we may boldly speak the Word and proclaim the gospel (Acts 4:19; Col. 4:3). He looses our tongue so we can boldly witness for Him and magnify and glorify His Name.

Open Doors Into the Glory World

But there are other doors in Scripture that Jesus has opened and does open for us. We find one of these doors referred to in Acts 7:56.

In this passage, we see that one of Jesus' disciples, Stephen, was being stoned to death. He became the first martyr of the Church. But the Bible has something interesting to say in this passage of Scripture about a door that Jesus opens for us.

ACTS 7:55,56
55 But he, BEING FULL OF THE HOLY GHOST, looked up stedfastly into heaven, and SAW THE GLORY OF GOD, and Jesus standing on the right hand of God,
56 And said, BEHOLD, I SEE THE HEAVENS OPENED, and the Son of man standing on the right hand of God.

This passage says that Stephen was full of the Holy Ghost. When Stephen was full of the Holy Ghost, he saw two things. He saw the glory of God, and he saw the heavens open and Jesus standing at the right hand of God.

Hallelujah! Thank God, God opens the door of Heaven for His people (Rev. 4:1). And one of these days God will open the door of Heaven to welcome you and me home. Whether we go by the route of the grave or by the Rapture of the saints, one day we are going home to Heaven to be with Jesus!

You see, there is a glory world. Stephen saw the glory of God. The psalmist of old said, *"Thou shalt guide me with thy counsel, and afterward receive me to glory"* (Ps. 73:24). That's where we are going when we leave this earth, praise God! Believers are going to the glory world!

I don't know about you, but I've been there; I've seen that glory world. I know what it means in this verse when it says that Stephen saw the glory of God.

Several times in the Old Testament when the people praised and worshipped the Lord, the Bible says that the glory of the Lord filled the temple.

For example, the cloud of the Lord's glory filled the tabernacle in the wilderness, and Moses could not enter the tabernacle by reason of the glory of God.

> **EXODUS 40:34,35**
> 34 Then a cloud covered the tent of the congregation, and the glory of the Lord filled the tabernacle.
> 35 And MOSES WAS NOT ABLE TO ENTER INTO THE TENT OF THE CONGREGATION, because the cloud abode thereon, and THE GLORY OF THE LORD FILLED THE TABERNACLE.

Then when the Israelites dedicated Solomon's temple, the cloud filled the temple, and the priests could not stand because of the glory of the Lord.

> **1 KINGS 8:10,11**
> 10 And it came to pass, when the priests were come out of the holy place, that the CLOUD filled the house of the Lord,
> 11 So that the priests could not stand to minister because of the CLOUD: for THE GLORY OF THE LORD HAD FILLED THE HOUSE OF THE LORD.

> **2 CHRONICLES 5:13,14**
> 13 It came even to pass, as the trumpeters and singers were as one, to make one sound to be heard in praising and thanking the Lord; and

when they lifted up their voice with the trumpets and cymbals and instruments of musick, and praised the Lord, saying, For he is good; for his mercy endureth for ever: that then THE HOUSE WAS FILLED WITH A CLOUD, even the house of the Lord;

14 So that THE PRIESTS COULD NOT STAND TO MINISTER BY REASON OF THE CLOUD: for the GLORY OF THE LORD had filled the house of God.

What was that cloud of the Lord? It was the glory of God — the cloud of the Lord's Presence — filling the temple. The Jews called the glory of the Lord the divine Shekinah or the Presence of God. The Presence of God dwelt in the Holy of Holies and it filled the temple.

I've seen that cloud of the Lord's glory. I saw it the first time as a teenager. Death came to fasten its grip on me at 1:30 in the afternoon on August 16, 1933, when I was just a teenager.

I had died once before as I lay on that bed of sickness before I was born again. I wasn't saved the first time I died, so when death fastened its awful grip on me, I descended down to the gates of hell.

Then God spoke from Heaven, and I supernaturally ascended back into my body.[1]

That was the day I got born again. After I was saved, I knew if I died, I would go up to Heaven to be with Jesus. So when I began to die that day in August, I said to my nine-year-old brother who stood by my bedside, "Run and get Momma. Quick! I'm dying. I want to tell her good-bye."

It was 106 degrees outside that day, yet my body was so cold that they had to wrap heated hot-water bottles and heated bricks all around my body to try to keep me warm. But my body was still as cold as ice all over, and the death dew was upon my brow.

My little brother ran out of that room calling, "Momma! Momma! Granny! Ken's dying!"

As he ran calling for Momma and Granny, I left my body. I was saved; I knew Jesus, so I went up, and I saw the glory of God. I heard a Voice speak from Heaven. I saw the glory of God!

The glory is brighter than the sun shining on the glistening snow. It is impossible to describe just how bright and beautiful the glory of God really is.

Years later, Momma heard me preaching on the radio about this experience of seeing the glory of God. One day when I came to visit her, she said, "Son, there is something about that experience you don't know about. There's more to it than you tell. Let me tell you about it from the standpoint of what Granny and I experienced."

She said, "When your brother Pat came running to us to tell us that you were dying, we ran out of the kitchen up the hall through the dining room to your bedroom. I was closer to the hall than Granny, so I got to your bedroom first. The door was open, and I started to run through that door. But I ran up against something, just like you would run up against a rubber wall."

She said, "I ran up against whatever it was that filled your room, and I just bounced back like I'd run into a giant rubber ball. I bounced back halfway into the dining room. I knew there was something holy in your room because your whole bedroom was filled with a bright light."

I answered, "Yes, that was the glory of God. My room was filled with God's glory."

She said, "I just bounced off it when I tried to run into your room, so I stood back in reverence. Granny came running up right behind me, and she ran up against it and bounced off too. But she backed up halfway into the dining room and ran against it again just as hard as she could.

"She couldn't get past that door! Every time she tried, she'd just bounce back. In fact, she tried about a half dozen times to get into your room, but she couldn't. Finally she just hung onto the door facing, barely able to stand up because of the Presence of God in your room.

"We both stood there about ten minutes before we could even get into your room. Whatever was in there, we had to wait until it had subsided and left before we could go into your room."

Well, you see, I was caught up in the glory of God. I couldn't see Momma or Granny; I was in that glory world! I've thought about it many times since then, and I have never felt sorry for Christians who leave this world. I feel sorry for those who are left behind, and I weep for them.

But I know this much. When I was caught up in that glory, I didn't want to come back. However, the Lord still had a work for me to do, so I had to come back.

Stephen saw that same glory. Then he saw Jesus standing at the right hand of the Father. Thank God, "He that openeth" opens the door of Heaven for His saints to usher them into that glory world! We'll all be welcomed home by Jesus one of these days.

Thank God for the door of salvation. Thank God for the door of divine healing and health that is open to us. God opens the door of our hearts, and He opens the Word to us.

Thank God, doors of service and opportunity and the door of utterance are open to us if we only have the spiritual awareness to see, recognize, and enter through those doors.

The windows of Heaven can be opened upon our lives down here on earth so we can live in abundance and be a blessing to mankind wherever we go.

Are the windows of Heaven open in your life? Have you entered into every door of blessing that Jesus has already provided for you?

Thank God, the door of Heaven will one day swing wide open to receive each one of us who are born again!

But doors of opportunity await you now, here on earth! May you see the blessings of the Lord poured out in your life as you walk through God's bountiful doors of blessing in obedience to His Word.

---

[1] For a complete account, please *see* Rev. Kenneth E. Hagin's book, *I Went to Hell*.